D0520434

HORIZON

SPRING, 1967 · VOLUME IX, NUMBER 2

Man of Many Causes

PETER SALADINO

Rudofsky

Bernard Rudofsky, whose article on troglodytes begins on page 28, is an architect, engineer, critic, designer, and inveterate traveler. He is also a malcontent who has ruffled more than his share of people by harping on the less-than-appealing aspects of twentieth-century life. As a result, many of his fellow architects openly consider him a traitor to his class; Yale University hired him as a visiting professor and then vetoed one of his lectures as too controversial; the State Department insists on listing his birthplace as Czechoslovakia on his passport, even though in 1905 it was part of Austria; and *The New Yorker* persists in describing him as a nudist because he once put together a museum show demonstrating how impractical modern clothes are.

Actually, that's precisely the trouble with Rudofsky. Instead of concentrating on the really important problems of modern life, such as the impact of ideology on space travel, he keeps jabbing away at the sacrosanct fundamentals of national identity: the food we eat, the shape of our shoes and chairs, our unsanitary methods of personal hygiene, and the utter failure of architects to anticipate the emotional requirements of the people who will inhabit their buildings and cities.

Architecture, of course, is his first love-hate. A graduate of Vienna's Polytechnical University, he was a practicing architect there and in Berlin, Naples, Milan, and São Paulo until 1941, when he and his wife, visiting New York at the invitation of the Museum of Modern Art, were marooned by World War II. When three years later the museum presented his unorthodox exhibition "Are Clothes Modern?" he left the question unanswered, except for some broad clues, such as the definition of the neologism "sartoriasis" as the enjoyment of discomfort.

A logical extension of his unconventional thesis—a sweeping indictment of American mores, manners, and monuments—was published in 1955. "The author's title for this book is *Uncle Sam's Cabin*," he complains on the first page. "Due to circumstances beyond his control, it is called *Behind the Picture Window*." Changing the title, however, did little to disguise Rudofsky's distaste for native cookery ("blasphemy"), home life ("drab"), and even the American bathroom ("indecorous").

Rudofsky's latest book, *The Kimono Mind* (selections from which appeared in HORIZON's Spring and Winter issues in 1965), is a thinly veiled comparison of life in this country and Japan. Its argument—and the basic premise in his

HORIZON is published every three months by American Heritage Publishing Co., Inc.

PRESIDENT
James Parton

EDITORIAL COMMITTEE
Joseph J. Thorndike, *Chairman*
Oliver Jensen
Richard M. Ketchum

SENIOR ART DIRECTOR
Irwin Glusker

SENIOR EDITOR, HORIZON
Marshall B. Davidson

PUBLISHER, HORIZON
Paul Gottlieb

Editorial and executive offices:
551 Fifth Avenue, New York, N.Y. 10017.

EDITOR
Joseph J. Thorndike

MANAGING EDITOR: Charles L. Mee, Jr.

ARTICLES EDITOR: Robert Cowley ART EDITOR: Jane Wilson

ART DIRECTOR: Kenneth Munowitz

ASSOCIATE EDITORS: Shirley Tomkievicz, Robert S. Gallagher, Barbara Klaw

ASSISTANT EDITOR: Priscilla Flood EDITORIAL ASSISTANT: Charles Folds

COPY EDITOR: Mary Ann Pfeiffer *Assistant:* Joan Wilkinson

ADVISORY BOARD: Gilbert Highet, *Chairman*, Frederick Burkhardt, William Harlan Hale, Jotham Johnson, John Walker

EUROPEAN CONSULTING EDITOR: J. H. Plumb, *Christ's College, Cambridge*

EUROPEAN BUREAU: Gertrudis Feliu, *Chief, 11 rue du Bouloi, Paris 1er*

HORIZON

A Magazine of the Arts

SPRING, 1967 · VOLUME IX, NUMBER 2

cultural canon—is that a civilization or nation best expresses itself and its ideals through its public and private architecture—and is, in turn, shaped by it.

Rudofsky has spent most of his life pursuing and studying architecture around the world and through the ages. There is little that escapes his eye, whether it be the lost grandeur of stairs (America's contribution, he wrote in the Autumn, 1964, issue of HORIZON, consists of fire escapes, "entrails of houses shamelessly flung over walls and windows alike") or the social impact of highways (HORIZON, February, 1962), from the multilane roads that spiraled up the Tower of Babel to the acres of asphalt and concrete now obliterating the landscape.

We have, by now, come to expect the unexpected from this iconoclastic observer, who always leaves us wondering what foible, what artifact, what societal impulse will next draw his critical ire. We put the question to him over the *mousse au chocolat* recently, and were immediately greeted with a brief soliloquy on the connection between juvenile delinquency and contemporary "vandal-proof" architecture. Later, as we parted on East 44th Street, he was still expounding the artistic merits of Turkish cemetery sculpture. He promised we would hear from him again soon—and so will our readers. R.S.G.

All correspondence about subscriptions should be addressed to: HORIZON Subscription Office, 379 West Center St., Marion, Ohio 43302.

Single Copies: $ 5.00
Subscriptions: $16.00 per year in the U.S. & Canada; elsewhere, $17.00

Annual indexes for Volumes I–VIII are available at $1 each. A cumulative index for Volumes I–V is available at $3. HORIZON is also indexed in the *Readers Guide to Periodical Literature*.

The editors welcome contributions but can assume no responsibility for unsolicited material.

Title registered U.S. Patent Office

Second-class postage paid at New York, N.Y., and at additional mailing offices.

History

TWO THOUSAND YEARS OF WAR IN VIET-NAM — *Bernard B. Fall* 4

LOST: THE TROJAN WAR — *M. I. Finley* 50

THE TWILIGHT PRINCESS AND THE SUN KING — *Joseph Barry* 106

Art

NEWS OF ART
- Michelangelo Pistoletto 84
- Andrew Wyeth's Portraits 86

THE ELEMENTAL TURNER — *John Canaday* 88

WHERE IS THE BRIDEGROOM? — *Gilbert Highet* 112

Architecture

TROGLODYTES — *Bernard Rudofsky* 28

A PLACE TO PLAY 42

Ideas

KONRAD LORENZ — *Edmund Stillman* 60

Letters

CRUSOE'S ISLAND — *Peter Quennell* 66

WILLA CATHER, "THE MEATAX GIRL" 116

The Contemporary World

CAN YOU BELIEVE YOUR EYES? — *Henry Fairlie* 24

DE MORTUIS — *J. H. Plumb* 40

Entertainments

ENGLAND, THE MELTING POT — *David Lowe* 56

FRINGE BENEFITS — *William K. Zinsser* 120

COVER: J. M. W. Turner's *The Fighting Téméraire Tugged to Her Last Berth* is probably his most popular picture. A detail appears on our cover; the full painting (left) now hangs in the National Gallery, London. The warship was in Nelson's fleet at Trafalgar. An article on Turner begins on page 88.

Two thousand years of war in

VIET-NAM

From the time of the ancient warrior to the modern GI, Viet-Nam has struggled to preserve its ancient land and culture from destruction

By BERNARD B. FALL

Men have borne arms in Viet-Nam since history began. The earliest known predecessor of the American infantryman above is the bronze warrior opposite, sculptured at Dong-Son in the second century B.C.

MUSEE GUIMET, PARIS; OPPOSITE: WIDE WORLD PHOTOS

There once was a country called Viet-Nam, at the eastern rim of the Southeast Asian mainland where it abruptly terminates in a balcony jutting out into the South China Sea. Significantly, German geographers called the area *Hinterindien* ("Beyond-India") and left it at that; but as early as 1812, Malte Conrad Bruun, a Danish-born geographer working in Paris, recognized the essential characteristic which made it different from the rest of Southeast Asia—the intimate mixture of Indian and Chinese civilizations. It was Malte-Brun (as he was known) who gave the area the name "Indochina."

To be sure, the part of Indochina that is now called Viet-Nam (it has carried various versions of that name—Dai-Viet, Annam, Nam-Viet—for more than a thousand years) has not disappeared from the maps as a geographic location. It is still there, the size of New Mexico, stretching out like a very elongated "S" for more than a thousand miles from just north of the equator to the twenty-fourth parallel. The Vietnamese like to think of their country as dragon-shaped, dragons being considered luck-bringing animals.

It is Viet-Nam as a cultural and historic entity which is threatened with extinction. While its lovely land has been battered into a moonscape by the massive engines of modern war, its cultural identity has been assaulted by a combination of Communism in the North and superficial Americanization in the South.

Viet-Nam's location has made it not only a melting pot of cultures but a battleground for foreign armies and foreign ideologies. The history of the South has been shaped by the kind influence of the Buddha; that of the North, where China has always prevailed, by the far sterner philosophies of Confucius and Lao-tse. And as far back as history and mythology can recall, the Vietnamese have fought among themselves, though maintaining a surprising amount of cultural unity. Many remains of a long and glorious past, which had withstood the inroads of dozens of invasions and which archaeologists had lovingly preserved, have now disappeared without a trace.

Like much of surrounding Southeast Asia, Viet-Nam was cut off from the rest of the world by the huge Himalayan glaciers of the ice age. The earliest traces of civilization are the so-called "choppers"—sharpened stones which were used as tools—dating back to 12,000 B.C. The first specifically Vietnamese culture emerged around 5000 B.C. in the caves and grottoes near Hoa-Binh, in what is now North Viet-Nam. "Hoabinhian" man belonged to the Australoid group moving from Central Asia southeastward into Indonesia and Australia; he may have been as dark-skinned as the present-day Melanesians of New Caledonia and the Solomon Islands. By 2000 B.C. a second wave of Australoids, armed with double-edged axes, entered the country on their way south. They are known as Bacsonians, after the Bac-Son area north of Hanoi where their remains have been mostly found. They

COLL. OF THE NATIONAL PALACE MUSEUM, TAIWAN, REPUBLIC OF CHINA; OPPOSITE: COLL. BERNARD B. FALL

China, the Constant Threat

The great power to the north of Viet-Nam has been a military menace since 111 B.C., when Viet-Nam was turned into a Chinese province. A thousand years later the Vietnamese broke free, only to become a prey to the Mongols. The effigy of a Mongol rider opposite is a reproduction of a thirteenth-century original made by the Vietnamese to commemorate their victory over fierce hordes from the north.

The kingdom of Champa, in what is now South Viet-Nam, usually found it wise to pay tribute to the Chinese. The arrival of a Cham embassy in the Chinese capital was recorded in the painting at the right by a T'ang dynasty painter, Yen Li-Pen, in A.D. 631. The emissaries arrived with offerings of elephant tusks, a mountain goat, a vase, and some pieces of petrified wood from the sea.

slowly spread throughout Southeast Asia, from Malaya to the Philippines, and became the first "Vietnamese" to settle the country permanently.

The third wave from Central Asia brought many of Southeast Asia's present inhabitants, in the form of the first Malays, who settled Java, Malaya, and the coastal area of Viet-Nam from Saigon to what is now the imperial city of Hué. The newcomers brought with them cattle, some metals, rudimentary irrigation, and upright stones, or megaliths, which have a striking resemblance to similar monuments found in places as distant as Europe and Easter Island. In Viet-Nam they also left magnificent burial chambers at Sa-Huynh (near Quang-Ngai, where American troops fought bitter battles last year with the Viet-Cong), and near the rubber plantations of Xuan-Loc and Bien-Hoa, just northeast of Saigon.

But around 1000 B.C. a new flood of people began to emerge from Central Asia: the Han Chinese. Endowed with a strong social organization, a sophisticated writing system, an advanced knowledge of agriculture, and, even then, an incredible propensity to multiply, the Han rapidly overran the small kingdoms that covered China south of the Yangtze. Like the moraine off a glacier, this new layer of humanity began pushing down the narrow Indochinese funnel into Southeast Asia. Until recently archaeologists felt that much of Viet-Nam's Bronze Age culture, particularly the beautiful finds at Dong-Son (see statue, page 5), was "imported" from the Han civilization about 500 B.C. But one of the most brilliant of the new generation of French researchers, Bernard Philippe Groslier, suggests that part of the Dongsonian culture may have been indigenous to Viet-Nam. Archaeological diggings by North Vietnamese at Thieu-Dong, a few miles from Dong-Son, in 1960–61, seem to indicate as much. They uncovered a Bronze Age culture of fifty-five graves and more than five hundred objects predating Dong-Son. The correctness of their findings will have to be verified by outside researchers, since the theory of an "autonomous" Vietnamese Bronze Age culture owing nothing to the Chinese suits Vietnamese nationalism on *both* sides of the seventeenth parallel. With Dong-Son, Viet-Nam entered the civilized world as we know it. Beautiful bronze statuary and huge drums of clearly Dongsonian origin began to show up throughout Southeast Asia and as far away as the Indonesian archipelago and the western Pacific. By the third century B.C. the Han invaders had driven the small kingdoms of South China into tight beachheads on the China Sea; they were also threatening Dong-Son. But the Dongsonians did not give up easily. Pushing southward, they entrenched themselves in snug little deltas surrounded by almost impenetrable jungle, and became the forerunners of the great Hinduized Champa kingdom.

One of the kingdoms of the Yangtze region defeated by the Han in the third century was that of the Vietnamese. (The Chinese ideogram for them was *Yuëh*, pro-

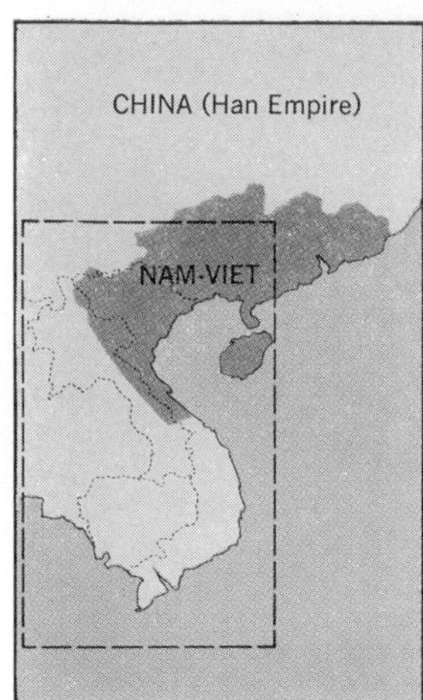

The First Viet-Nam—111 B.C.

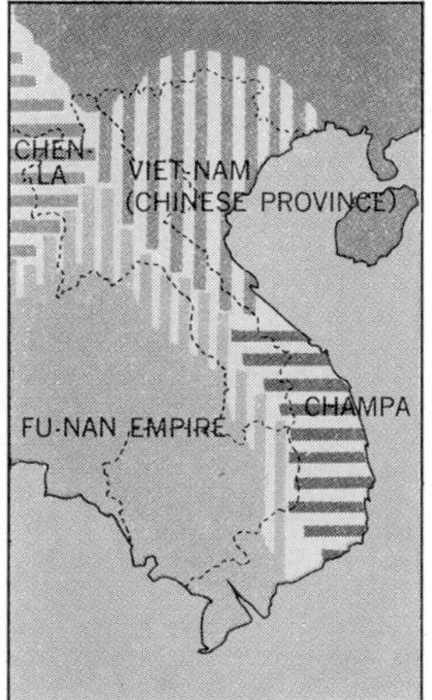

Fifth-century Kingdoms

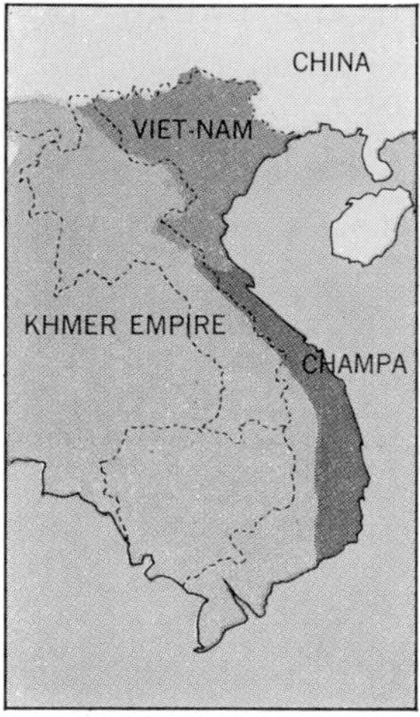

Twelfth-century Indochina

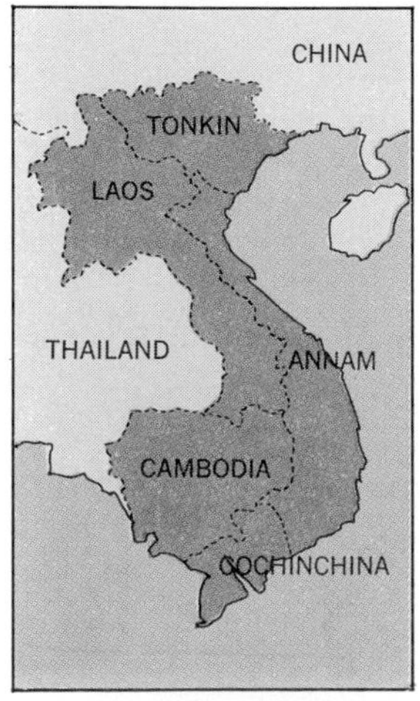

French Indochina 1883–1941

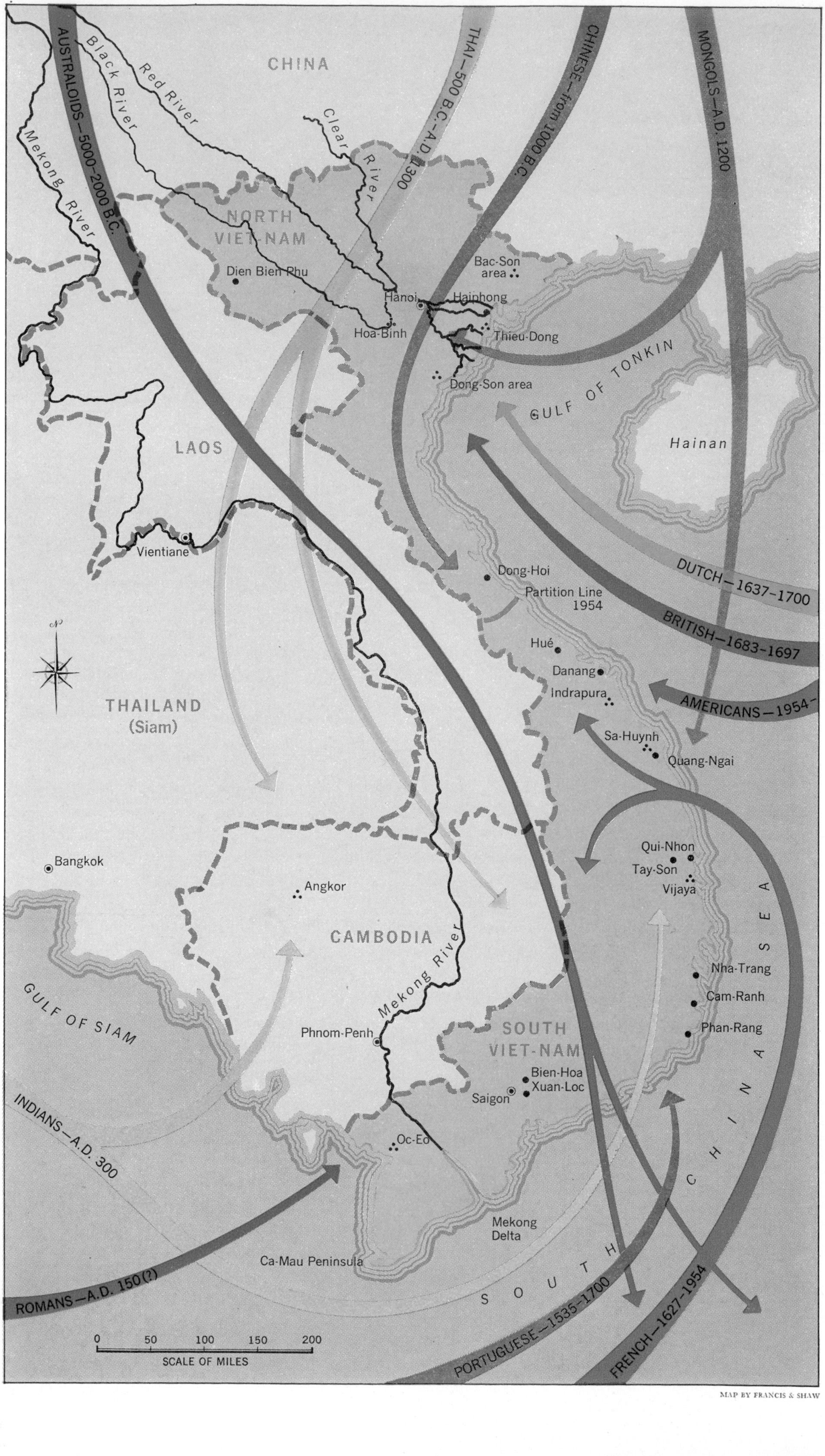

MAP BY FRANCIS & SHAW

nounced "Viet" by the Vietnamese.) As the Han advanced, the Vietnamese retreated southward. By 257 B.C. we begin to encounter the first formal diplomatic correspondence between the pursuer and the pursued. But a country as huge as China was hard to keep together, especially since the advance element of settlers (as was often the case in Western colonization efforts) was made up of convicts, adventurers, and other rough-and-ready types. Occasionally they would strike out on their own or would even join the opposition. That was the case with a Chinese front-line general by the name of Chao-T'o (Trieu Da, in Vietnamese), who conquered the Vietnamese in 207 B.C. and proceeded to install himself as king of the country—which by then comprised a small part of what is now North Viet-Nam.

The Empress of China immediately proclaimed a complete blockade of Viet-Nam, forbidding in particular the export of such "strategic" items as iron plowshares and of female draft animals. The principal effect was to stiffen Vietnamese resistance. When Trieu Da changed his title from king to emperor, matters seemed to be rapidly coming to a head. But in the end the essential wisdom of the rulers prevailed. Han Wen-ti, the emperor who succeeded Empress Lu in 179 B.C., sent an ambassador to Trieu Da with a diplomatic note whose text—fortunately preserved for posterity—would do no dishonor to any future negotiator of the Vietnamese problem:

> Respectfully to the King of Nam-Viet. I am most distressed in my heart and afflicted in my thoughts . . . I have learned that you have recently sent troops to the border to pilfer and ravage. Not only did the Trang-Sa [area] suffer, but [your] Southern Command suffered even more. Under such conditions how could even your Kingdom derive a single advantage from this? Surely, a great many officers and soldiers will be killed, many excellent generals and officials will be wounded; wives will be deprived of their husbands, children of their parents, parents of their offspring. To gain one and lose ten—I do not consent to act like this. . . .
>
> You are ruling in full independence; yet you have changed your title to that of Emperor. When two Emperors exist at the same time and no ambassadorial chariot establishes connections between them, struggle will ensue. But to struggle unyieldingly is not a deed for men endowed with humanity. Let me then share with you, and forget, our earlier differences . . .

The old Vietnamese king promptly replied that all that had happened was just a terrible "misunderstanding" and that he had made himself emperor, as the French translation says, "*quelque peu pour se divertir*"—as a lark. Trieu Da reaffirmed his vassalage to the Chinese emperor, changed his title back to king, and sent a tribute of white jade, bird plumage, and rhinoceros horns. This arrangement settled Sino-Vietnamese relations for more than half a century, with the only penetration of Chinese culture being a peaceful one.

Meanwhile another phenomenon, which to this day is the key to all Vietnamese attitudes, came to the surface—a violent internal struggle between those who felt that good relations with China, even at the price of vassalage, was important, and those who felt that Viet-Nam would soon become nothing but a Chinese province if it tolerated the Sinicization of its every cultural trait, from its language to the manner in which rice was irrigated. Unfortunately that controversy developed at the height of one of China's expansionist phases, when it was trying to achieve both a common border with India and a broad bastion on the Pacific: in 111 B.C., after a brief campaign, the Chinese overran the young Vietnamese state. Three years later they occupied Korea. The Chinese occupation of Viet-Nam was to last, with a few brief interruptions due to rebellions, for 1,050 years, until A.D. 939.

At the same time, in what is today South Viet-Nam, a more peaceful penetration from India and points farther west was taking place. Bulging out into the South China Sea, South Viet-Nam has always been a welcome stopover for sailors on the China trade routes, and it was not surprising that many of its early colonizers came by sea. In the South, mythology and history abound with tales of Indian princes and Buddhist monks alighting from big sailing ships and bringing to the primitive populations of the lower Mekong the enlightenment of their advanced civilizations in addition to the liberal teachings of the Buddha.

Strangely enough, there are no contemporary Indian texts available to us about the kingdoms they established in Southeast Asia. But the Chinese, ubiquitous traders, travelers, and diplomats that they were, have again left us detailed descriptions of the opulent cities which then dotted what they called the kingdom of Fu-Nan—its Indian name being unknown—located in the South Vietnamese Mekong Delta and southern Cambodia. Historians viewed some of the Chinese texts with disbelief until French aerial surveys of the 1930's and 1940's revealed the patterns of hundreds of elaborate canals and of vast cities grouped around them like so many Venices. It may have been at this time that the first Europeans reached

The Dragon-shaped Land

The historical map opposite shows the various peoples who have come to Viet-Nam, some in peace and some with arms, some for brief stays and some for permanent settlement. Major cities and the important archaeological sites are also indicated. Political boundaries of Indochina at four different points in history are sketched on the small maps at left.

The Legacy of India

The men of India came to Indochina on civilizing missions, bringing their great religions and art to the Cham kingdom as well as to the more famous Khmer empire in what is now Cambodia. Unfortunately the Chams went to war against the Khmers in 1066. In the detail of a Khmer relief from the ruins at Angkor (opposite) two Cham warships sail into battle, as Khmer foot soldiers march in the register above them. The Chams were defeated and went home, only to be attacked by the Vietnamese some three centuries later.

At left is a ninth-century Cham statue of the Hindu god Siva. At right is a Khmer version of Siva's consort, Paravati, who stops her ears in order to avoid her husband's commands.

Viet-Nam. Whether or not Romans actually visited the port city of Oc-Eo has not been clearly established, but the fact remains that a Roman coin dating to Antoninus Pius (A.D. 152), and Sassanid brooches have been found there, along with thirty other clearly Roman objects. There is little doubt, in any event, that by the third century A.D. Oc-Eo had become a crossroads of civilizations. Here Chinese ships deposited their merchandise and passengers to be picked up by Indian ships bound westward; and here they picked up cargo and travelers seeking to find their way to the huge and mysterious Chinese empire. Chinese records also show that in the middle of the third century A.D. the first Indian missionaries, seeking to spread the gospel of Buddhism eastward, stopped over in Fu-Nan before going on to Canton. The rulers of Fu-Nan soon recognized the power of the great nation to the north, and like the Vietnamese, paid a nominal tribute to China.

But to the east of Fu-Nan and south of the kingdom of Viet-Nam, a new power was emerging—Champa. The Chams, who were mentioned by the Chinese for the first time in A.D. 192, were the Norsemen of the South China Sea. Their raiding ships preyed upon the slow, unsuspecting Chinese trading junks—emerging from veritable "fjords" whose names sound familiar even today: Danang, Qui-Nhon, Nha-Trang, Cam-Ranh, Phan-Rang. Fu-Nan, peaceable and unprepared for war, became an easy target for the raiders. By the end of the sixth century, Fu-Nan had disappeared altogether, and the beautiful cities around Oc-Eo, sacked and destroyed repeatedly, began to sink into the mud of the Mekong. Where they once were, there are now a few "strategic hamlets" in the midst of abandoned rice fields seared by napalm and crop-killing chemicals. But for almost a thousand years after its disappearance, Christian chroniclers would spin tales about the marvels and riches of Transgangetic India or the Golden Chersonese. What they were looking for were the golden cities of South Viet-Nam.

Now it was Champa's turn to become a regional trade center. Cities like Khautara (Nha-Trang), Panduranga (Phan Rang), and Indrapura were known to Arabic seafarers from Baghdad and India, and were in regular touch with Java and China. After numerous wars in which they gave as good as they got, the Chams also decided that it was the better part of wisdom to pay a symbolic tribute to China and to exchange periodical embassies with her (see page 7). Toward the eighth century a truly magnificent culture blossomed out along what is now the shore of northeastern South Viet-Nam. Champa, however, was afflicted with the same drawback as seafaring powers such as Portugal and Holland: it had to rely on trade even for its food and was constantly vulnerable on its land side.

Such was the fate of Champa in the face of the progressive inroads of the Viets. Internal troubles in China had resulted in a gradual weakening of its power, and

ABOVE RIGHT: LEONARD VON MATT—MUSEE GUIMET, PARIS

The Coming of the Westerners

The first European depiction of an Indochinese landscape was the miniature above, painted in France in 1351 to illustrate the journals of a Franciscan missionary who had traveled through the peninsula. He was especially impressed with the land of Champa—where the very fish of the sea, he averred, paid homage to the great Cham king. The natural wealth of Indochina had attracted even the Romans. Whether their ships ever ventured that far east is uncertain, but in 1944 a cache of Roman coins was found at the ancient port of Oc-Eo, west of Saigon. Among them were the two shown opposite: a gold coin of Antoninus Pius, minted in A.D. *152, and one of cornelian, incised with a portrait.*

The seventeenth century was the heyday of European traders in Viet-Nam. The English print opposite, right, shows Hanoi ("Cha-Cho, the Metropolis of Tonqueen") after the English and Dutch had established trading posts there. Their flags fly above two warehouses at the right of the city.

Viet-Nam had liberated itself from the Chinese yoke. Like their other neighbors, however, the Vietnamese had learned a useful lesson: a small state cannot long exist on the Chinese periphery in a condition of permanent hostility. The result had been an offer of tribute and a renewal of a relationship of loose suzerainty. Aside from a brief period of Chinese occupation in the 1400's, that would be the relationship between the two until the late nineteenth century, when the French took over.

With the Chinese mollified, the Vietnamese rulers turned their sights southward. There the Chams had let fertile agricultural land lie fallow in their preoccupation with trading, raiding, and building temples, while the already teeming Vietnamese had been constricted to their lowland deltas in the Red River region. What began now was a nasty episode of colonialism with overtones of genocide. The Vietnamese began to destroy the Cham state piecemeal, city by city and province by province. By the end of the fifteenth century Champa had not only disappeared from the map but almost all its population had disappeared as well. Today a few ruins and about fifty thousand Indonesian-looking *montagnard* people, who now follow the Moslem religion of their blood brothers in Malaya and Indonesia, are all that survives of that once proud kingdom.

Even the physical remains of the Chams are disappearing under the pounding of war. Last fall a *New York Times* correspondent visited a small open-air museum

Iconographie de l'Indochine francaise, 1931; LEFT: MARILYN SILVERSTONE, MAGNUM—NATIONAL MUSEUM, SAIGON

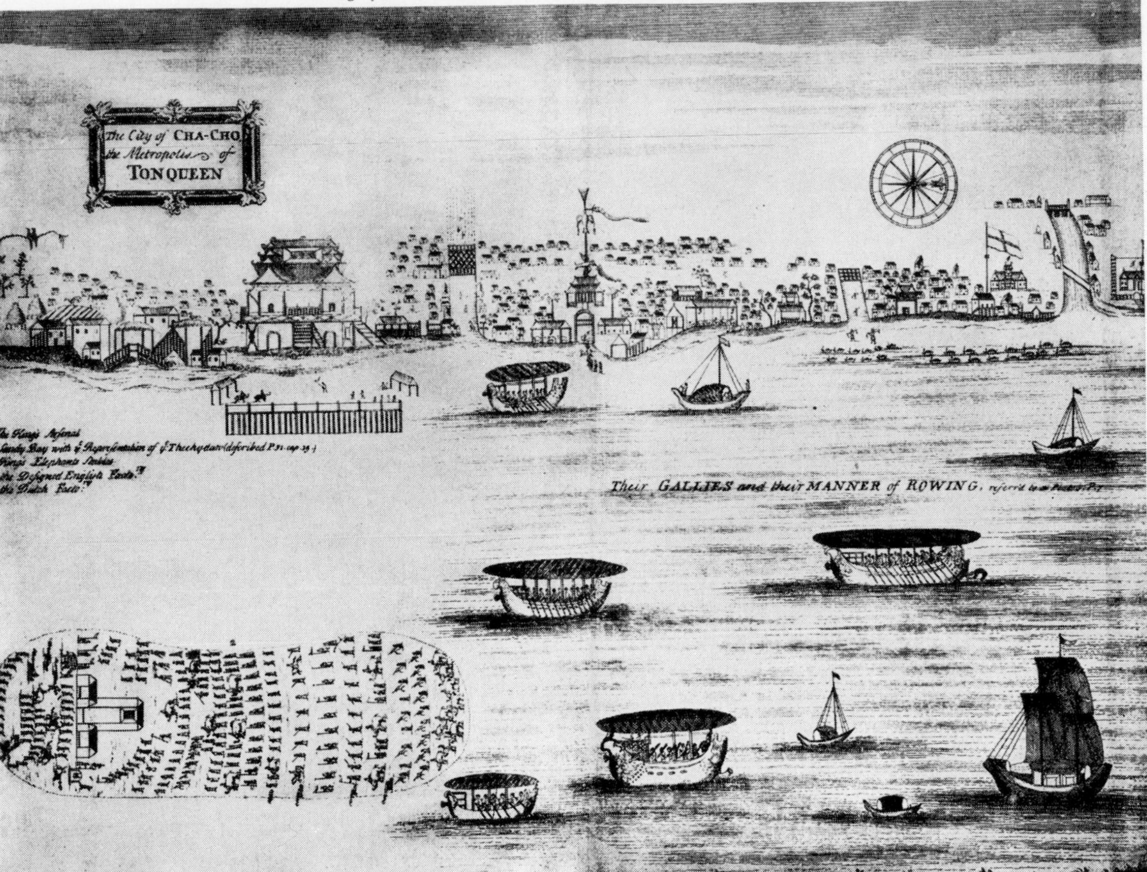

near Danang which the French had built to house Cham relics. He found it littered with "bat droppings, American beer cans, and rusty C-rations tins . . ." During the Buddhist uprising in May, 1966, snipers had used the museum as a sanctuary; while little damage had been done to the building itself, the heads of three of the museum's statues had disappeared.

The Vietnamese had embarked upon their own version of the Chinese Long March, and even had a war cry: "*Nam Tiên!*" ("Let's March South!"). Yet, as Groslier noted with a tinge of regret, "that vigorous movement was only the triumph of demography—not of a civilization." The Vietnamese carried south with them a thoroughly Sinicized civilization, and it suited them so well, intellectually, administratively, and artistically, that they showed little incentive to change it.

There was one trait that the Vietnamese had not borrowed from the Chinese—their enduring patriotism. It was to be put to a severe test many times in their turbulent history, but probably never to a greater one than when, a tiny nation of perhaps a million people, they stood up to the mighty Mongol empire.

Peking had fallen to the Mongols in 1215. By 1257 the first Mongol invasion—contemporary figures speak of 200,000 men—flooded the Red River valley. The Vietnamese, as they would so often do later, abandoned their cities and headed for the hills, leaving their capital to be burned by the invaders. But the Mongols, still unused to the tropics and tropical diseases, were defeated by the environment; after a fruitless pursuit of the Vietnamese, they withdrew. A few years later, Kublai Khan made a second attempt at crushing Viet-Nam, not because he needed the backwater kingdom on the Gulf of Tonkin, but because it blocked the overland route to Champa, which the great Khan wanted as a naval base for further operations in Southeast Asia. Marco Polo left us a description of the campaign against what he calls "Ziamba," which took place about 1268 after a landing by sea and left the Vietnamese in the center of a Mongol pincer.

In 1284 the third Mongol invasion of Viet-Nam began. At first there was an understandable feeling of hopelessness as once again the Mongols ravaged the lowlands; more acclimated now, they were less likely to be dislodged by climate alone. That was the moment when a great military leader and thinker stepped forward: Marshal Tran Hung Dao. He withdrew to the mountains, wrote his *Essential Summary of Military Arts*, and began to train his troops in what we now call guerrilla warfare. His principles could just as well have been written by Mao Tse-tung or Dao's present-day successor in Hanoi, General Vo Nguyen Giap, the victor of Dien Bien Phu: "The enemy must fight his battles far from his home base for a long time . . . We must further weaken him by drawing him into protracted campaigns. Once his initial dash is broken, it will be easier to destroy him."

Missionaries from France

Frenchmen originally came to Viet-Nam as missionaries and traders, not conquerors; but French political interests were greatly advanced by Pigneau de Behaine, the enterprising bishop, at right, who solicited French military aid for Prince Nguyen Anh (later Emperor Gia-Long) in staving off a civil rebellion. Accompanying Pigneau to the court of Louis XVI was Nguyen Anh's young son, Prince Canh, whose portrait, left, was painted at Versailles.

The French did not attempt a real political take-over until much later, provoked in part by such incidents as the massacre of 1840 depicted in the Vietnamese painting opposite. At the top, three Catholic missionaries from Tonkin are led in procession with iron stanchions and chains; in the center of the painting they are decapitated.

And that is exactly what happened. In 1287, after the Vietnamese had whittled down the Mongols through protracted guerrilla warfare, the latter decided to withdraw. Tran Hung Dao planted thousands of iron-spiked stakes in the Bach-Dang river north of Haiphong through which the Mongol fleet had to pass. The ships arrived at high tide, when the stakes were submerged. A small Vietnamese naval force cleverly decoyed the enemy into a fight which looked like an easy victory until the Mongol ships found themselves stranded or gored on the stakes by the momentum of the outflowing tides. That was the moment Marshal Dao's infantry chose to attack and defeat the invaders.

But once more wisdom prevailed: the following year Viet-Nam voluntarily offered to pay tribute to the Mongols in Peking. A last Chinese invasion under the Ming emperors, in 1407, was eventually defeated by the same mixture of guerrilla and attrition warfare, and a new dynasty of Vietnamese kings, beginning with Lê Loi in 1418, reigned until the end of the eighteenth century.

With no dangerous enemies left, the Vietnamese settled down to what seems to be their favorite national pastime: bitter quarrels among themselves in general, and between Northerners and Southerners in particular. In the North the Lê kings had fallen under the spell of powerful feudal lords; in the South the Nguyen feudal family had for all practical purposes taken control. By 1613 the "two Viet-Nams" had not only broken apart but the South had constructed at Dong-Hoi its own version of the Great Chinese Wall. In fact there were two walls, one six miles long and the other twelve, both of them eighteen feet high. Dong-Hoi is only a few miles north of today's division at the seventeenth parallel.

But this was the great epoch of European trade and colonial expansion, and the arrival of the Westerners further complicated the split. Thanks to the more modern arms which became available, it also made the conflicts between North and South more deadly. To be sure, the contact with Europe from Marco Polo's time on had never been broken, but trade had proved unrewarding. The Dutch, who had opened a trading station in North Viet-Nam (see page 13) as early as 1637, lost two fleets of warships when they helped the Lês fight the Nguyens in several disastrous campaigns; they finally closed up shop in 1700. The British tried in 1683 and quit in 1697. The French opened a trading post in 1680 and closed it in 1682. With all of India and China and the Spice Islands for the picking, the European merchants turned their eyes and capital elsewhere.

Not so the Catholic missionaries. To them, the Vietnamese, with their mélange of Confucianism, Taoism, ancestor worship, and remnants of Hinduistic beliefs, were ripe prospects for conversion. On January 18, 1615, the first Italian and Portuguese Jesuit missionaries landed in what is now Danang, and their initial successes led the

PAINTINGS MISSIONS ETRANGERES, PARIS

MUSEE DE LA FRANCE D'OUTRE-MER, PARIS

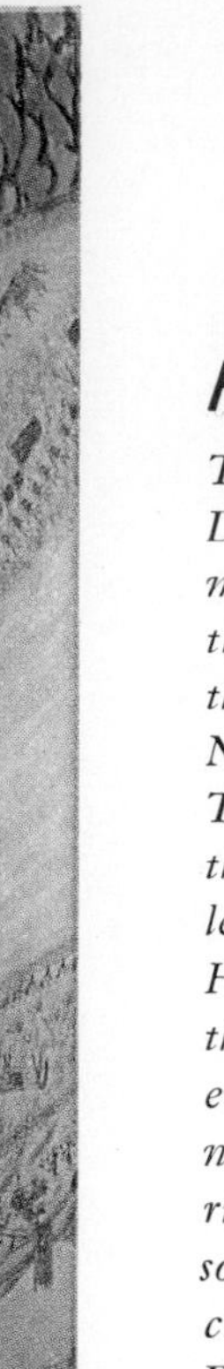

France Acquires a Colony

The landing of French forces at Danang in 1856 was the opening move in a sporadic power struggle that did not end until 1884, when the French finally subdued all Viet-Nam and drove the Chinese out of Tonkin. A Chinese artist painted the bird's-eye view of a battle, at left, which took place in 1884 near Hanoi. French troops, occupying the two forts at the top, are covered by gunboats against the Chinese infantry advancing along the riverbanks. The city of Hué, to the south, had fallen in 1883. Its mighty citadel, opposite, was fortified by French engineers in the early nineteenth century. The great enclosure, which protects the imperial palace, is almost two miles square.

pope to send a permanent mission to Viet-Nam, headed by a French Jesuit, Alexandre de Rhodes. Monsignor de Rhodes remained there for twenty-two years, and by the time he was banished in 1649, tens of thousands of Vietnamese had embraced Catholicism. But Rhodes had done more than that: he had transliterated Vietnamese from the Chinese characters to the Latin alphabet, with the adjunction of a few diacritical marks to account for the multitonal character of the Vietnamese language. A door had been forced open which would never close again.

In the meantime the Nguyen had taken over the Long March southward, moving into the Mekong Delta. But they, in turn, were to be faced with the rise of a "Third Viet-Nam" at their backs—just as a hundred and eighty years later the Viet-Cong was to divide Viet-Nam into three areas. In 1771 three brothers from Tay-Son village in the South rose against the Nguyen with demands for social reforms and reunification. They found a ready echo among the landless peasants oppressed by their feudal lords, and among the merchant class, distressed at the loss of internal as well as foreign trade because of the country's division. Soon, all the Nguyen rulers save one young prince, Nguyen Anh, had been murdered, and by June, 1776, the Tay-Son were masters of most of South Viet-Nam.

Two years later the Tay-Son had defeated the tottering Lês and their supporters in the North. Only Nguyen Anh, holed up in the Mekong swamps or sometimes fleeing to neighboring Cambodia and Siam, still held out against all hope. In his despair the young prince approached the French bishop in the Mekong area, Pigneau de Béhaine, and persuaded him to go to France to secure help from the French king, Louis XVI. France, a short while earlier, had won a war over Britain (and with it, the independence of the American States) and had footholds in India; perhaps she would be willing to help a young Asian ruler as well.

In 1784 Monsignor Pigneau embarked for France, taking with him Nguyen Anh's son, four-year-old Prince Canh, who became the darling of Versailles. But in spite of a treaty of assistance signed in 1787, France, bankrupt from wars and cracking under the stresses of oncoming revolution, could do very little. The governor of French India, Count Conway, sent four warships to Viet-Nam in August, 1788, which returned with a pessimistic report on the chances of Nguyen Anh's success. Undeterred, Monsignor Pigneau and the young Prince Canh sailed from France with a single privately bought warship and three hundred French volunteers attracted by the promise of land. They landed in Viet-Nam in mid July, 1789, the week the Parisians stormed the Bastille.

Incredible as it may seem, the tide was eventually turned by this minute infusion of modern military know-how, coupled with the fact that the Tay-Son were now more preoccupied with another Chinese invasion in the North and had neglected to deliver on promised reforms.

RAYMOND CAUCHETIER

WERNER BISCHOF—MAGNUM

But the overthrow of the Tay-Son was a long and arduous process. Not until July, 1799, did Qui-Nhon, the key Tay-Son fortress in the South, fall, after a brutal siege which Monsignor Pigneau personally directed. He had only a few months to enjoy his victory. He died in October and was followed to the grave a year later by his pupil, Prince Canh. Nguyen Anh proceeded to exterminate the Tay-Son leaders, and by 1802 had crushed the movement from north to south. A few years later he made himself emperor under the name of Gia-Long. For the first time in almost two centuries Viet-Nam was a single country, from the China Gates in the north to the Ca-Mau Peninsula at its southernmost tip.

The influence of the small group of Frenchmen who had come with Monsignor Pigneau waned as rapidly as their small numbers were depleted by disease or homesickness. But two of them had an influence which to this very day has not been wiped off the Vietnamese landscape: Théodore Lebrun and Olivier de Puymanel. They were both military engineers, and their star-shaped forts soon dotted the landscape—for Gia-Long had ordered the construction of a citadel in every provincial capital and at other strategic points. Above all, Gia-Long wanted a modern port city in Cochinchina, and from 1789 to 1792, Lebrun and de Puymanel laid out a modern city in the south, with broad rectilineal boulevards facing a protected river habor where there once was a fishing village called Saigon. When Gia-Long died, in 1820, Viet-Nam not only was a consolidated state but was secure and prosperous; it had even incorporated what was left of Cambodia. It is to Gia-Long that Vietnamese hark back when they dream of their country's greatness.

Gia-Long's successors, however, did not match their ancestor in realism and intelligence. Rather than face up to the realities of growing European intervention as Siam and Japan were reluctantly doing, they attempted a retreat into isolationism and began to expel Western merchants and to persecute Christian missionaries and converts. Figures vary, but the best-documented sources show that about 130,000 Catholics, including hundreds of priests and several important church dignitaries, were murdered between 1827 and 1856. The largest single persecution of Christians since Nero, it goes far to explain the present-day distrust between Catholics and Buddhists in South Viet-Nam.

It was the persecution of the Catholics which brought about the first documented intervention of American military force in Viet-Nam. The old U.S.S. *Constitution*, under the command of Captain John ("Mad Jack") Percival, was showing the flag in Asian waters when he was informed that the Vietnamese were about to put to death the French bishop Dominique Lefèbvre in Hué. Percival put in to the nearest Vietnamese port, Danang, on May 10, 1845; he marched a Marine detachment ashore, captured several high Vietnamese officials (who no doubt did not even know that America existed), and held them

WIDE WORLD PHOTOS

HOWARD SOCUREK, *Life* MAGAZINE, © TIME INC.

The French Heritage

The mark of France is not likely to be effaced from South Viet-Nam. The three women at far left, part of a Catholic population of two million, come daily to pray in their village church. Saigon, which was laid out in the 1790's by French engineers, retains a definitely Parisian look, and many shop signs, like that of the "bijouterie" at left, are still in French. One of the bitterest moments of French defeat in Indochina occurred on October 9, 1954, when French troops lowered the tricolor at Hanoi headquarters (right) for the last time. They then abandoned the city they had held for seventy years, the last eight of which had been spent in a futile and exhausting war.

hostage until, four days later, Hué assured him that the bishop would not be harmed. When Washington later found out what had happened, it was properly appalled, and in 1849 sent its consul at Singapore to the court at Hué to apologize. It is doubtful that a single one of the Marines who waded ashore at Danang in 1965 had an inkling that his appearance was a return engagement.

The French who landed in Danang in 1856—ostensibly to save the Catholics from persecution—and then secured Saigon and the surrounding Mekong Delta in the following decade, knew that there had been Frenchmen there before them. But this time they came to stay as a colonial power, convinced that they were bringing enlightenment as well as progress and the benefits of colonial commerce. Often the errors made at the beginning when two civilizations collide—whether it be that of the French and Vietnamese in the 1860's or that of the Americans and the Vietnamese a hundred years later—fatefully condition the whole development of the relationship. That was to be the case now. Since the late fifteenth century, Viet-Nam had elected its local governments and this had proved an effective shield against the imperial government's highhandedness. "The Emperor's writ stops at the bamboo hedge [of the village]" is an old Vietnamese saying. The arriving French colonials began to tamper with those hallowed institutions, thus breaking one of the most important links in Vietnamese society. The French, unfortunately for themselves, understood this too little and, above all, too late; but it took the incredible blindness of the late Ngo Dinh Diem to abolish local elected government altogether. When he did so, in 1956, the Viet-Cong had the issue it was looking for. Appointed village chiefs were killed by the thousands, and the first round of the second Indochina war went to the opposition by default.

The French colonial government probably did no better or worse than most colonial governments. A university was established in Hanoi as early as 1904; vast irrigation systems eliminated the disastrous floods or droughts which had beset Viet-Nam's agriculture and transformed the country into one of the world's food baskets; and epidemics were completely wiped out by a network of Pasteur Institutes. But the French failed to provide the Vietnamese with a real say in the political development of their country, allowed too few of them to obtain an advanced education and too few of them to rise high in the administrative hierarchy of their own country. French-type cities gave the country a veneer of Westernization beneath which a small but vigorous intellectual class grew increasingly impatient with the colonial framework.

One result was the growth of the secret societies that had always been part of the Sino-Vietnamese civilization. This is a phenomenon largely unknown to us: in the West, only Communism is specifically geared to operate as a clandestine political party. It was a combination of

A Tormented People

Brightly garbed Buddhist monks, whom government troops have ringed with barbed wire, staged a street demonstration in Saigon last summer to protest against the military regime. At right, a young Catholic girl and her neighbor hobble away from their battered village.

HORST FAAS—WIDE WORLD PHOTOS

WIDE WORLD PHOTOS

Marxist ideology and the secret societies of Viet-Nam that produced the *one* effective political organization the country has ever had—the Indochina Communist Party, later known as the Vietnamese Workers' Party under its creator, Ho Chi Minh.

For those who refused that alternative but were reluctant to work with the French, there were only two choices: exile or an escape into meditation and religion. It was France's best expert on Vietnamese society, Professor Paul Mus, who once spoke of "*le goût du merveilleux*" —the "hang" for the supernatural—of the Vietnamese people. In the 1920's and 1930's this gave rise to new religions such as the Cao-Dai, a mixture of spiritism and a type of ecumenical Buddhism in which Christ, the French poet (and atheist) Victor Hugo, and Winston Churchill, have a fitting place.

During the Second World War both the French and Vietnamese settled down to living with their Japanese masters. The latter turned out to be even less willing to understand the inhabitants than the whites were; but they brought to the Vietnamese a chance to shake off the French yoke. The Japanese collapse, however, left a total void, and the only group which was not only willing but also capable of taking power in Viet-Nam was the Viet-Minh, which included Communist as well as non-Communist nationalists under the leadership of Ho Chi Minh. His Democratic Republic of Viet-Nam, proclaimed on September 2, 1945, returned Viet-Nam, how-

Crossroads of the Orient

Having retained something of all the peoples who have tramped across it, Viet-Nam is a land of bewildering contrasts. The gong beaters at left belong to a primitive tribe of the central highlands of South Viet-Nam. They live more or less like their ancestors, who arrived in the prehistoric period. Saigon, on the other hand, has every modern urban headache, including traffic jams. Its streets are choked with private cars, U.S. Army trucks, jeeps, pedicabs, motor scooters, and innumerable bicycles—the most popular mode of transportation.

ever briefly, to the ranks of independent nations; but the return of the French and the divisions among the Vietnamese Nationalists made a conflict almost unavoidable.

Last-minute efforts in 1946 to head off the oncoming Indochina War failed as French and Viet-Minh moderates were swept aside by the extremists in both camps. As the war ground on, a new division of Viet-Nam began to take shape: the French, and the Vietnamese regime under their control, held all the cities and towns; the Viet-Minh held the villages and the jungle. The French lashed out in ineffectual "search-and-destroy" operations, but the Viet-Minh, following Marshal Tran Hung Dao's doctrine, refused to be drawn into a major battle. Finally, the French offered them 17,000 troops in the valley of Dien Bien Phu as "bait," just as the Mongols had attempted to corner Dao in the plain of Bach-Dang. In a grueling fifty-six-day fight the Viet-Minh won. It was a victory of Communism, to be sure, but it was also a victory of which every Vietnamese would henceforth be proud, just as Americans, regardless of where their personal sympathies lie, are proud of Gettysburg.

But unlike Gettysburg, which insured the eventual reunification of the United States, Dien Bien Phu sealed the division of Viet-Nam into a northern Communist and a southern non-Communist state; their cultures would soon diverge under the competing influences of Russian and Chinese training in the North and American training in the South. In both zones the French cultural overlay flaked off under the impact of new techniques and, in the South, of a far more massive influx of foreigners than the country had ever seen and one which it simply could not absorb. In the North common poverty at least insures that the living standards of the urban areas are not markedly different from those of the countryside. In South Viet-Nam the cities have become the home of incredible traffic jams—an American wag has baptized Saigon "Honda-ville"—and the social decay that attends war. Meanwhile the countryside literally dies under the blows of the largest military machine ever unleashed on an area of this size. And in that blistered countryside lives the "Third Viet-Nam"—the Viet-Cong and its northern allies, who hide in deep underground burrows, as if returning to the Stone Age cultures of Hoa-Binh and Bac-Son.

It was in 1931, after yet another abortive rebellion against the French, that a young Vietnamese author and poet, Pham Quynh, told the French colonial minister, Paul Reynaud (who would be France's premier in the dark days of June, 1940): "We are a people who are looking for a country and have not yet found it." Thirty-six years later that search still goes on, more desperately than ever.

Bernard B. Fall, a Frenchman and Professor of International Relations at Howard University, is in South Viet-Nam on a Guggenheim grant. His latest book, Hell in a Very Small Place, *is about the battle of Dien Bien Phu.*

U.S. NAVY
EA-5202

Can You Believe Your Eyes?

None of us has ever seen Alexander the Great emerging from his tent. If there had been television in his day and we could look at the tape, would we know him any better, as we think we now know a John F. Kennedy or a Lyndon B. Johnson when we see them, on television news, emerging from a convention?

None of us has ever heard Julius Caesar speak. But if there had been radio in his day and we could listen to the recording, would we know him any better, as we think we know something important about Franklin D. Roosevelt from his fireside chats?

The answer is far from clear. Of all historical evidence, the public presence of voice or of physical appearance is the most revealing but can also be the most misleading. Yet the problem of historical evidence is raised every night on television news, when we are asked to accept what we see and hear as genuine. It is raised especially by the two most important television news programs in the United States: Huntley-Brinkley on NBC, and Walter Cronkite on CBS. Millions of people have to decide not so much whether they can believe what they are told but whether they can believe what they see flickering in front of them.

"The evidence of their own eyes": but that is precisely what is not available to them. What *is* available is the evidence, first, of the camera, making its own selection, dictating its own terms; and it is the evidence, then, of the small screen—still the best description of television—which in turn dictates to the camera. Can television, by its nature, ever tell the truth?

Amid all the pretentiousness of his theorizing, Marshall McLuhan is right to this extent: the medium is the message. Television does not merely create news. That is an old business, practiced for generations by newspapers. Television creates its own events, something even the most imaginative newspaper reporter cannot do. The newspaperman can only create words, and however powerful they may be, words do not *happen* over the breakfast table as television *happens* in a living room. Thomas W. Moore, ABC's president, came very near to the point when he said: "It is difficult to retain one's perspective when, without leaving the security of our living rooms, we become witness to such startling events as the assassination of an assassin, or a war in progress."

It is because television *happens* in this way that people begin to think that the small excerpts from life which they see on the screen in their living rooms are more "real" than the life which they experience around them. There is a vital margin of difference between saying, "Did you see the report in *The New York Times* of the massacres in the Congo?" and saying, "Did you see the massacres in the Congo on television last night?" The first remark implies only that one has seen a report (which may conflict with a report from another source). The second implies that one has seen the event itself. However carefully television is used, it cannot avoid this deception.

It is doubtful whether it is ever easy—sometimes whether it is ever possible—for a newspaper or television reporter to report an event. He can report incidents, and it is the nature of incidents that they can, and do, happen in isolation. But the true meaning of an event depends on all of its known and unknown causes, on all of the known and unknown incidents that contribute to it, and in the process, cease to be isolated, and on all of its known and unknown repercussions. The whole of an incident can easily be described; the whole of an event may escape even the historian.

If this is a difficulty that confronts the newspaper reporter from day to day, it is one that the television reporter can rarely overcome. For the newspaper reporter possesses a flexibility that the television reporter does not have. He has flexibility because he can move without the paraphernalia and encumbrance of a camera or a camera crew. He has flexibility because he can reach where the camera cannot reach: the camera can never go "off the record."

The newspaperman has flexibility, above all, because words are flexible and the length of a story is flexible: the one able to qualify, even in the shortest parenthetical expression; the other capable of imposing its own perspective. But however carefully chosen the words of a television reporter, they can never properly qualify a spectacular picture; and however discriminating the apportionment of stories in a television program, they are in length too nearly the same.

Incidents are usually in the open; the whole of an event, often obscure and private. Not only is the core of television the public and the spectacular, but there is an important sense in which television has a vested interest

On television the news happens in front of you. But is that what really happened? Is it a true picture or only a violent episode? Would it have happened at all if the TV cameras hadn't been there? *By* HENRY FAIRLIE

in disaster. From the point of view of a good story, both newspapers and television prefer covering a major strike to negotiations which prevent a strike. But it is possible for the newspaper reporter to make negotiations almost as exciting a story as a strike itself: by word of mouth, he can collect a picture of the comings and goings which are the essence of negotiation and, by his words in print, vividly describe them. But what can television do with negotiations? It can only show pictures of people arriving at a building and people leaving it. However colorful they may be—and the modern business executive is not normally colorful—this does not make exciting viewing.

Violence is the stuff of television, and the question of how to deal with it is the most important one confronting the medium.

To be sure, the same question confronts newspapers; but the impact of violence—whether a boxing match, a riot, or a massacre—is much greater in a moving picture than in a still picture or in descriptive prose. Violence is movement—the raising of an arm, the smashing of it on someone's head—and movement is what television cannot help emphasizing.

In covering violent situations, three distinct characteristics of television conspire to intensify both its special problems and the special temptations to which it is exposed. There is, first, the limitation of time. A lead news story in a paper such as *The New York Times* may take twenty minutes to read; in a popular newspaper or a tabloid, as many as ten. There simply is not this time available in television news. In the reporting of all news, this means concentration to the point of distortion. In the reporting of violence, it means concentration on the violent incident to the exclusion of the whole event.

An outstanding example of such distortion was the police attack on civil rights marchers at the Selma, Alabama, bridge in March, 1965. I was not present myself. But I do not know one reporter who was present, and whose opinion I trust, who does not point out that there was first a prolonged period during which police and demonstrators faced each other, without violence, in an atmosphere of unbearable tension, and who does not agree that the tension had to break in the form of police action.

Television news—except in special features and documentaries—did not, and could not, show this preliminary encounter. Three minutes of film is an extended sequence in a news program, and the time is best filled with action, not inaction. On the other hand, a single phrase in a newspaper story, placed correctly, where it carries weight, can put even an extended description of violence in perspective.

The point of such perspective is not to excuse any eventual police brutality, but to explain it. Without this explanation, whether implicit or explicit, one begins to think that brutality is automatic, that the police will always behave in such a manner; demonstrators begin to think that they can, and should, goad the police; and the police begin to think that, since restraint is so frail anyhow, they may as well give way to exasperation from the start.

There is, secondly, television's tendency to produce self-generating news. The problem arose most notably during the disturbances in Watts; but it has arisen, again and again, whenever there have been similar disturbances in other cities. However spontaneous the original outbreak of violence, an external provocation is added once it has occurred. That provocation is the presence of television cameras in the middle of the trouble spots.

This is especially true on the night after the original outbreak. Then, as dusk gathers, television cameramen and reporters move into the streets looking—literally looking—for trouble, and the crowds begin to play up to them. Their presence is very different from the presence of newspaper reporters, who either roam around, hardly distinguishable, or lounge in bars until they hear that action has broken out somewhere down the block. Television, merely by its presence, helps to create incidents and then itself remains part of the happening. There is no doubt that this participation occurred after the first night in Watts, and that it occurred again last summer in Chicago.

But in order to create on the screen the impression of continuing disturbance, of continuing riots, television needs only one incident. One spectacular incident of violence can occupy a two-minute sequence in a news program just as impressively as a series of incidents. Much of the Watts film is a classic example of this: showing that it needs only one defiant boy and only one hot-headed policeman to suggest that a neighborhood is aflame.

In this connection it seems worth pointing out that a newspaper reporter's dishonesty—or imagination—can be a great deal less dangerous and provocative than a television reporter's. The newspaper reporter, after all, need only create—or exaggerate—a story in his own mind. But the television reporter must create—or exaggerate—it in actuality: he must make it a happening.

Finally, in this matter of violence, there is the size of the screen: the limitations which it imposes, the temptations it offers. At the end of last summer, television news showed some alarming pictures of white men and women in the Chicago suburb of Cicero screaming abuse at some Negro marchers. Their hating faces—a dozen of them, perhaps—filled the screen. They looked as if they were a representative example of a much larger crowd. But anyone who was there knows that these particular whites were only a small part of the crowds in the streets; and that the crowds themselves were only a small part of the total white population of Cicero. To this vital extent, television that night distorted badly.

What all this amounts to is not only that people sitting in their homes begin to think that all police are brutal, that all demonstrators are violent, that all disturbances are riots, that all crowds are aggressive; the fact that they usually go through each day without either meeting or themselves displaying violence becomes less real to them than the violence on the small screen.

Anyone who has appeared regularly on television knows that complete strangers think they have actually met him. They smile or nod at him in the street or across bars; they approach him and shake his hand; they even ask him to drop in when next he is around their way, as if they really believe that he has been in their homes. It is this imaginary "real" presence of television in people's living rooms which is the background to the whole problem. Surely much of the feeling of living in a condition of perpetual crisis, and the agitation arising from it, comes from a sense of being a witness to a world which is more actual than the routine world in which one lives.

Television can create, not only events out of incidents, but movements and people. The television news coverage of the Meredith march across Mississippi, during the couple of days when I accompanied it myself, constantly appalled me. It was near the beginning of the march, when it had barely gotten organized, and when the numbers were few and the individuals composing the numbers were anything but impressive.

All the familiar hazards of television reporting were displayed. A straggling column—it was at the time little more—could be made on the small screen to look like an army. When the cameras were rolling, the marchers pulled themselves together and played the role expected of them. The several civil rights leaders strode in line abreast, at the head of their enthusiastic followers.

WIDE WORLD

The real story of the Meredith march was not this unified demonstration at all, but the fact that it produced the deeply significant clash between different factions of the civil rights movement over "black power." Newspapers felt their way to this story and were, by the end, reporting it fully. It was a story which, for the most part, was taking place in private meetings where the cameras could not reach. But then when television at last caught on to the fact of "black power," it inevitably exaggerated and distorted it. Film is expensive. Getting film ready for a news program is a hurried job. The result is that in reporting any speech the television reporter and cameraman make an automatic, almost involuntary, selection. They wait for the mention of a phrase like "black power," and on go the lights and the film rolls.

But, given the length of the usual sequence in a news program, that is all. The impact is far greater than that of any selection made by newspapers. By constant reiteration on the small screen day after day, the slogan of "black power" was elevated into a movement. It was suddenly there. It had suddenly happened. "Black power" switched the cameras on, and in turn the cameras switched the movement on. It was a classic case of self-generating news.

Stokely Carmichael, of the Student Nonviolent Co-ordinating Committee, could not have emerged so rapidly as a national figure without television. (SNCC is a master at using television.) But he is not the only example of television's ability to create—or destroy—people. No one, I think, questions that Governor Ronald Reagan is the creature of the television cameras, just as previously Actor Ronald Reagan was the creature of the movie cameras. John Morgan, one of the British Broadcasting Corporation's most experienced television reporters, returned from the California gubernatorial campaign last fall, amazed at Reagan's professionalism in the television studio, and the use that he made of it to dictate camera angles and even the moments for close-ups.

Much of the poor impression that President Johnson has often made is the direct result of his comparatively poor television "image." The close-up, especially, can distort in the crudest way and make what is simply unprepossessing actually repellent. In fact, in considering the impact of the close-up, one can notice the vital difference between television and the movies; between what is legitimate in the cinema and illegitimate in a living room.

Movies are intended to be, and are taken to be, larger than life. Sitting in the theatre, one does not imagine that what one is seeing is real. The close-up in the movies, therefore, is a legitimate *and understood* distortion. But a distortion it is. We never do see anyone in real life as close in as the camera can go, except in one position and in one activity: when making love. There is no reason why President Johnson, or any other public figure, should have to pass this private test in public. Moreover, not only does the close-up bring one ridiculously close to a face, it shows it in isolation. It removes the general bearing; it removes the whole man.

Perhaps the most striking demonstration of the power of television to create personalities is one that most people will think also demonstrates its power for good. For a comparatively short time three men seemed to bestride the world: John F. Kennedy, Pope John XXIII, and Nikita Khrushchev. Their impact, all over the world, was quite out of proportion to the length of time any of them held office. In a few years they had made as great an impression as Queen Victoria had in sixty years. This was the work of television.

Television news is new, and we have not yet got the measure of it. Its hazards are numerous: some of them are inherent in the nature of the medium, and are likely to be permanent. Others are more technical and, with technical advances, may be removed.

Camera crews are costly, and costly to move about; this automatically imposes a preselection of news far more rigorous than it is in a newspaper. Film costs impose a second automatic selection. Time on the screen is expensive, and this imposes a final selection. Again and again, when I have been making news films with a camera crew, I have wanted to utter over the pictures, "It was not like this at all."

However paradoxical it may seem, the only immediate answer to most of the problems of television news lies not in pictures but in words. Given the powerful impact of the pictures, the words covering them must provide the corrective. Most television reporting just describes the pictures, and by doing so, reinforces them. But the object of words in television news should be to distract from the pictures, to say: "It was not quite so. This was not the whole story." Pictures simplify; the object of words should be to supply qualification and complication. Pictures involve; the object of words should be to detach the viewer, to remind him that he is not seeing an event, only an impression of one.

The manner of delivery—especially of the "anchor" men in the studio—is as important as the substance of the words themselves. There is something very professional and very engaging about the television manners of Chet

WIDE WORLD

Huntley and David Brinkley and Walter Cronkite. All of them, in dissimilar ways, cultivate a deadpan approach. In Huntley, it is made to suggest a judicial impartiality; in Brinkley, an ironical detachment; in Cronkite, an unfailing common sense. Each of them by his manner reinforces the impact of the pictures over which he is speaking, suggesting that they can be taken at their face value.

Only now and then, when Brinkley's irony is allowed to break loose into that overnourished flicker of a smile, is the value of the pictures ever questioned. The vital role of the television reporter or commentator is to make watching as difficult as reading, to invite the viewer to make comparisons and judgments from his own experience so that he never reacts by assuming that he is seeing actual life.

That television news can do some things remarkably well, especially in full-length features and documentaries, that those involved in making television programs are conscientious and skillful, does not touch the main problem. Television news holds a mirror up to the world in a way that newspapers never can; and the world is beginning to believe that it can recognize itself in it. Life is not made up of dramatic incidents—not even the life of a nation. It is made up of slowly evolving events and processes, which newspapers, by a score of different forms of emphasis, can reasonably attempt to explore from day to day.

But television news jerks from incident to incident. For the real world of patient and familiar arrangements, it substitutes an unreal world of constant activity, and the effect is already apparent in the way in which the world behaves. It is almost impossible, these days, to consider any problem or any event except as a crisis; and, by this very way of looking at it, it in fact becomes a crisis.

Television, by its emphasis on movement and activity, by its appetite for incident, has become by far the most potent instrument in creating this overexcited atmosphere, this barely recognizable world. The medium, to this very important extent, has become the message; and the message is perpetual stimulation, perpetual agitation, perpetual change. The world it creates is a world which is never still.

Many of our unnecessary anxieties about the way in which we live, about the fearful things that may happen to us, might be allayed if television news began, now and then, to say: "It has been a dull day. But we have collected some rather interesting pictures for you, of no particular significance." Television news has a deep responsibility to try to be dull, from time to time, and let the world go to sleep.

One of England's best-known political commentators and the man responsible for the term "Establishment," Henry Fairlie has covered upheavals from Cyprus to Mississippi for newspapers and television. He is now reporting the U.S. scene from a Washington base.

The cave dwellers of Cappadocia, in central Turkey, live in a landscape of veritable fairy-tale settings (opposite). Although the cones and hummocks that are their houses have been crumbling away for centuries, this has not stopped them from being used.

Troglodytes

Putting architecture underground may turn out to be the ultimate solution to provide adequate shelter for the man of the future

By BERNARD RUDOFSKY

ETYMOLOGICAL NOTE

Troglodytes: Latin *Trōglodyta*, from Greek *Trōglodutēs*, plural *Trōglodutai*, name of a race that lived in Ethiopia. The earliest known mention of them is in Herodotus, who may have heard of them during his travels in Egypt (c. 449 B.C.). He does not say that they lived in caves. He says only that they lived in Ethiopia, were hunted by the Garamantes, were very swift runners, and that their language sounded like the squeaking of bats. He gives the name as *Trōgodutai*, which is in all probability simply a Greek version of the "real" name of the tribe, whose language, and therefore the literal meaning of the name, is unknown.

However, this name in Greek by the addition of one letter can be made to mean "cave-dwellers," "they who enter caves"; *Trōglodutai*, from *trōglos*, cave, hole + *-dutai*, "they who enter," from *duein*, to enter. Coupled with Herodotus's remark that their language resembled the squeaking of bats, it was embroidered to the point of fantasy, and the name became a generic name of "weird cave-dwellers." It was so transmitted into Latin and modern languages. There is thus no reason to suppose that the original *Troglodytes* lived in caves, except for the fact that Greek imagination liked to think they did.

—Peter Davies, chief etymologist of the forthcoming AMERICAN HERITAGE DICTIONARY OF THE ENGLISH LANGUAGE

Paris-Match, FROM PICTORIAL

A civilization where practically everything is disposable, including civilization itself, has no room for relics. Things old and durable are looked upon with suspicion, if not with contempt. Even such a venerable institution as the house—the sort we frivolously call home—fails to engage our affection. The thought that a building constructed several centuries ago might still serve its original purpose is heresy to those who believe that progress is unavoidable, indeed irremediable. Today, when technological obsolescence has become the prime mover and prerequisite of progress, our buildings are wrecked long before they have outlived their usefulness. The life span of a house in midtown New York is progressively shrinking, while the eventual demolition of even the newest of its glittering skyscrapers is not so much a matter of time as of economy. And though conventional sentiment does tolerate the cult of ruins (no doubt because there are almost none in our country), the continued use and care of superannuated architecture abroad—not just of grandiose buildings but of humble houses as well—strikes us as absurd. Their very longevity is felt as a drag on the advancement of mankind. It follows, therefore, that that most indestructible form of shelter, the cave dwelling, must appear to our eyes the most despicable sort of habitation.

Perhaps it is the fact that most caves are gratuitously supplied by Nature that puts them beneath contempt. At any rate, since caves are not offered for rent or sale, the idea of inhabiting them never occurs to us. Despite the increasing unhealthiness of our surface life—the dangers compounded of mephitic air and polluted water, not to mention the ever-present dread of atomization—real-estate agents have so far overlooked some startling opportunities. So they go on peddling the brittle wooden crate, the plaything of floods and tornadoes, that promises no refuge from an angry Nature. Compared to the rock-bound cave, today's house is as precarious as a canary's perch—but we continue to insist that it is the best habitation yet devised.

It just happens that prejudice is stronger than fear or any practical consideration. To our way of thinking, caves are for cave men only; troglodytism—living in caves—amounts to disowning one's status as a human being. Still, we cannot deny that caves have served as habitations much longer than ordinary houses; and however repugnant to us may be the thought of living in a naked cleft of rock, caves have often been selected by man as a retreat from the intemperance of the weather and as a hiding place from his enemies.

The being whom we label, carelessly, a cave man (a vulgarism that usually stands for upper paleolithic man), was actually an outdoor type. Sportsman and naturalist, he led a nomadic life and probably used caves only for occasional shelter. To judge from the kind of litter he left behind—mostly meat bones and human skeletons—caves served him primarily for cookouts and burials. Unlike us, however, he did not memorialize the dead with tombstones or painted likenesses. A superb artist, fastidious and technically accomplished, he was mainly preoccupied with the animal world; among the herds of bison and buffalo that he so brilliantly portrayed on the walls of caves, the image of the human hunter amounts to little more than a shorthand symbol. Nor were still lifes or landscapes of interest to him; his painterly vision was Michelangelesque—a preference for the entanglement of robust, albeit brutish, bodies. Indeed, there is nothing facetious about calling Lascaux the Sistine Chapel of prehistory; the famous caves, it has been argued, were shrines rather than ordinary dwellings. Now the time has come to dispel the belief that all inhabitants of caves were, or are, subhuman rabble. Quite the contrary: the uncouth cave often attracted an elite such as rarely walked aboveground.

It is a sobering thought that Christ was born in a lowly cave, and that His word lived on because His disciples, literally, went underground. The grotto as a refuge pleasing to God has its precedent in the cave that concealed the infant Zeus, or in the one to which the Japanese sun-goddess retired, thereby plunging the world into darkness. Besides, anyone acquainted with the life and death of ancient Mediterranean nobility, terrestrial or celestial, cannot help bring struck by its taste for subterranean residences. Heroes, nymphs, and monsters alike

FOGG ART MUSEUM, HARVARD UNIVERSITY

Rome and Byzantium disagree over the setting of Christ's birth. The thirteenth-century Italian who painted the Nativity *above sided with the Eastern Church and placed the setting in the mouth of a cave rather than inside a shed.*

COMMISSARIAT GENERAL AU TOURISME

Cave dwellings range over wide areas of Mediterranean countries. The corridor above left leads into the chamber of the Cumaean sibyl, whose cave was hewn from the trachytic tufa of a hill that rises abruptly from the seashore at Cuma, near Naples. The ninth-century monolithic church at Saint-Emilion (above right), in the western part of France, was also carved, not "built."

made their home in the folds of the earth. Some of the most famous love matches were consummated in the intimacy of caves: Medea, the lady magician, took Jason in marriage in a cave at Iolcos; Odysseus dallied away seven years on the island of Ogygia as house guest of the cave-dwelling sea nymph Calypso; again, a cave was the classical setting for the union of Thetis and Pelias, of Dido and Aeneas.

Aeneas also figures prominently as guest of another notorious troglodyte, the Cumaean sibyl, Mother Divine of all seers, who preferred the beguiling cachet of a cave to more conventional lodgings. Her sanctuary near Naples consisted of a sort of crypt under the temple of Apollo, presumably built by the aviator-architect Daedalus as a token of thanks on the occasion of his successfully completed flight from Crete. (Aware as he was of the historical importance of his feat, he bequeathed his wings to the holy place, thus adding a touch of the Smithsonian to it.) Although outranked by Delphi—the Vatican of necromantic prophecy—the Cumaean sibyl's cave was a hotbed, if not of intellectualism, at least of divination, smoked and cured over a magic tripod. The words that issued from it seemed as portentous to the ancients as do the more expensive oracles of analysts and pollsters to us.

There was nothing lowly about that supernatural agency run by the sibyl. Its down-to-earth, rock-bottom rusticity was tempered by an aroma of saintly exclusiveness, perhaps because at one point of her career the seeress had been married to Apollo. Visitors to the premises were rattled by the sheer vastness of her cave, laid out as it was on the scale of a concert hall rather than that of a boudoir. According to Virgil, no fewer than one hundred entrances led to the oracle of the Cumaean sibyl, something that taxes the imagination of the most megalomaniac architect.

When the sibyl grew old (she had muffed her chance to ask Apollo for immortality) and her local prestige declined, she packed up her things and moved north. This expedient is not unique in the annals of the gods; Venus, alias Aphrodite, similarly prospecting for new spheres of activity, crossed the Alps into Germany where she found a suitable cave in the Hörsel mountain in Thuringia. However, an alien mental climate and the emergence of an uncompromising foe, the Church, obliged her to adopt novel methods of seduction. The way she conducted her most notorious affair, the temptation and conquest of the moody Tannhäuser, bears witness to her unabating resourcefulness. As even the most casual operagoer knows, she supplemented her charms with a *corps de ballet* and, to suit the Teutonic tastes of her lover, a full orchestra of heretofore unheard brassiness of sound and sentiment. Stifled by all this heavy-handed gaiety, Tannhäuser sought a change of air in a voyage to Italy. In Rome he confessed himself to the pope, who promptly refused absolution—whereupon the good knight returned to the enchanted cave to live happily ever after.

Even so, one would be well advised not to take up prolonged residence in Nordic caves. From the point of view of healthfulness, they are no better than dwellings aboveground. Whatever the purported advantages of living in a rude climate—the hardening of body and mind to the point of callousness—cold caves are no place for self-indulgence. For, whereas in a warm climate the temperature of subterranean spaces is nearly constant the year round, northern caves—we only have to think of New York's subway—are equally uncomfortable in summer and winter. Arthritis deformans, the bone disease that was epidemic, indeed endemic, in the ice age, afflicting cave man and cave beast alike, is still with us.

The fires that early man built in his cave were probably no more effective in dispersing cold and damp than our modern electric heaters. What kept the fires burning was the need for smoke, rather than warmth. Not only did smoke act as a disinfectant, but it preserved the stores of Stone Age larders: dried fruit, dried fish, and dried meat; it cleared the cave of vermin and of all animals with a lower coughing point than man. On the whole, though, troglodytic fauna held few terrors. The dragons and minotaurs soon departed from the scene, while scorpions, vipers, and poisonous spiders were never much to worry about. What ultimately marked the domestication of the cave was the appearance of domestic animals: a sweet smell of cow and donkey, similar to that of the Manger (before the Magi spiked it with frankincense and myrrh), pervaded the premises.

A nineteenth-century traveler visiting Tunisia, a country abounding with troglodytes from time immemorial, recorded these remarkable row houses, reached by rope ladders only.

ENTE NAZIONALE INDUSTRIE TURISTICHE

Besides serving as *pied-à-terre* for philandering gods, caves also accommodated a galaxy of demigods and their demimonde, as well as some of the great of the earth. In times when emperors were more numerous than they are today, tradition prescribed that they enhance their image with expensive building programs—when actually their private demands were on the frugal side and all they craved was a comfortable cave. The emperor Tiberius, to name but one, was an *aficionado* of underground apartments. He shared this taste with the Roman landed gentry, who placed their country seats in the vicinity of a *specus aestivus,* a grotto that promised coolness during the most torrid summer. Unfortunately these elegant cellars had one annoying drawback: the volcanic soil of Italy is prone to the ravages of earthquakes. Tacitus tells of a dinner party in Tiberius's cave, near today's Sperlonga (the name is derived from the Latin *spelunca*), when suddenly the roof gave way, burying a number of servants. The monarch himself remained unscathed, thanks to Sejanus, his chief minister, who had the presence of mind to throw himself over Tiberius, protecting him with his body.

Hermits of every philosophical and theological persuasion were another group with a distinct hankering for subterranean, or at least cavernous, quarters. Whatever their capacity for the self-denial of life's amenities, some kind of shelter was indispensable to their survival. Yet building a house, or even only a roof, they felt, might impair their unworldliness. Hence a natural cave—sometimes improved beyond recognition—afforded them just enough protection from the elements without compromising their vow of poverty. It satisfied their idea of unpropertied existence: they remain Nature's squatters.

The picture of the anchorite in front of his rocky lair, painted a thousandfold in the art of the Church, may not appeal to us. To our mind solitude fosters indolence and vice: meditation seems nothing short of consorting with the devil. Moreover, the recluse shirks competition, to us the foremost aim in life. Be that as it may, some hermits, confident that their instincts were sound, advertised in no uncertain terms the coziness of their caves. "O ye that dwell in Moab," counseled Jeremiah with his customary tendency to overstatement, "leave the cities, and dwell in the rock, and be like the dove that maketh her nest in the sides of the hole's mouth." No matter how good Jeremiah's judgment of cave dwellings, the dove

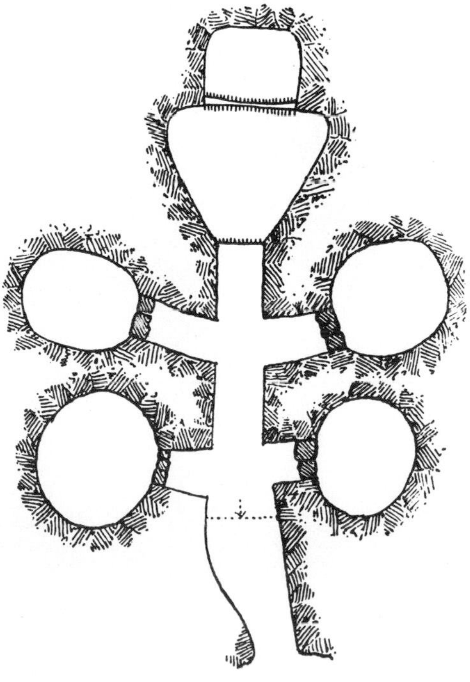

Thirty centuries ago the Siculi, a prehistoric tribe from the Italian mainland, carved a necropolis out of the cliffs of the Anapo Valley, near Syracuse in southern Sicily. In the Middle Ages, when the tombs were converted into multistoried dwellings, it became the town of Pantálica (now abandoned). At left is a floor plan showing a cluster of rooms.

instinct in man was then far more pronounced than it is today. The geographer Agartharchides, who lived in the second century B.C., filled fifty pages with descriptions of cave dwellers in the Red Sea region alone. Moreover, Palestine, Anatolia, Ethiopia, and the countries of the Mediterranean all the way to the Pillars of Hercules, were rich in natural caves. One modern geologist even speaks of troglodytic *nations*.

To be sure, these were no nations of Calibans. Not all of these cave dwellers affected the scanty dress of early man; they were probably indistinguishable from ordinary people. Perhaps their diet was—at least to our mind and palate—on the adventurous side. Ethiopian troglodytes, for instance, fed on serpents and lizards, or what we would call, disdainfully, "gourmet foods." Others, we are told, drew strength from drinking a mixture of milk and blood. But let nobody tell you that the prophets in the desert underwent culinary hardships simply because, as the Bible notes, they had to subsist on locusts. Not only is the taste of toasted grasshoppers exquisite, but one may gorge on them while appearing to undergo physical mortification.

As we said, cave-dwelling hermits are not necessarily misanthropes. Although conviviality would seem to defeat the very idea of self-imposed solitary confinement, history shows that reclusion is quite compatible with togetherness. The best example, a veritable apotheosis of troglodytism, is furnished by a former colony of monks and nuns in Cappadocia, a wild mountainous district in today's Turkey.* Since it has become accessible to the traveler in recent times, it may deserve special mention.

To the west of Erciyas Daği, the Mount Argaeus of the ancients, lies a volcanic region that is among the most picturesque in the world. The soil of the valleys supports orchards and vineyards of great fertility, while the conical hills are riddled with cavities eminently suited for human dwellings. The fame of the place rests on a gigantic housing project put up by Nature at her most magnanimous—but let us yield the word to one Paul Lucas, an emissary of Louis XIV who claimed to have been the first European to lay eyes on the extraordinary sight. "I was overtaken," writes Lucas, "by an incredible astonishment at the sight of some ancient monuments on the other side of the river [Kizil Irmak, or Red River, the Halys of the Greeks]. Not even now can I think of them without being struck. Although I have traveled a good deal, I never had seen or heard of anything similar—pyramids in prodigious number and of various height, each consisting of a single rock, hollowed out in a way as to yield several apartments, one on top of the other, with beautiful entrance doors and large windows for the well-lighted rooms."

Had Lucas fallen victim to an optical illusion, or did he merely suffer from the kind of travel euphoria that sometimes befogs the mind of the most sober observer? No, he had not: the pyramids were palpably real, although somewhat less perfectly shaped than Lucas's drawings would have us believe. For all we know, he may very well have made out doors and windows where others have seen but gaping holes, if only because he considered doors and windows the proper attributes of all grand architecture. Having taken a fancy to these *maisons pyramidales*, he mentally elaborated on their design. "I mused at length about the meaning and purpose of so many pyramids, for it was not just a matter of two or

* See "The Rock Monasteries of Cappadocia" in Winter, 1964.

The skyscrapers opposite are rock formations in Cappadocia (see pages 28–29). Formerly occupied by hermits, today they house wild pigeons. When the outside surfaces slid away, peasants walled up the exposed chambers, leaving holes for the birds whose droppings serve as fertilizer. At right is an engraving from Paul Lucas's Voyage dans l'Asie Mineure. *Lucas mistakenly thought the rock cones had been constructed by man.*

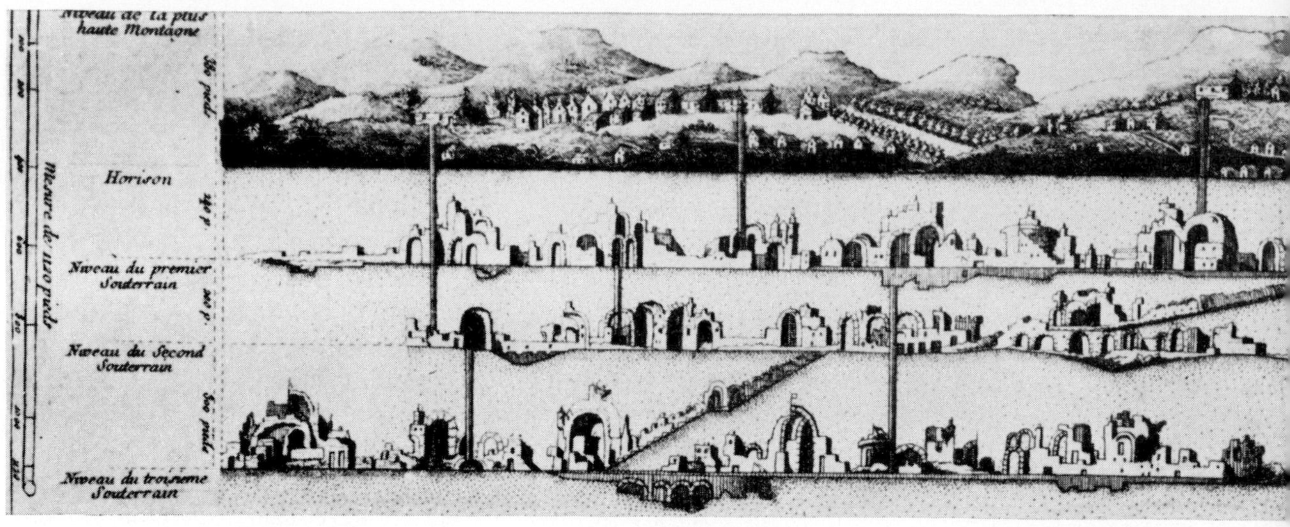

three hundred but of more than two thousand. Each of them terminated in a cowl or bonnet, shaped like those of Greek priests, or a female figure cradling a child in her arm, that I immediately took to be an image of the Virgin. Which gave me the idea that they once sheltered some hermits."

Alas, for all his perspicacity and imagination, Lucas was much akin to the hurried tourist of our day; he simply did not take the time to examine his discoveries. Darting to right and left as fast as the pace of his caravan permitted, he caught a few glimpses—through open doors—of mural paintings and archaic inscriptions, before, to his "mortal regret," an approaching band of highwaymen forced him to abandon his exploration. Little did he suspect that the caves contained acres of murals that some day would open a new chapter of Byzantine art.

At home Lucas's account of the Cappadocian cave dwellings was received with disbelief and his renderings were ridiculed. In his excitement he had quite pardonably exaggerated some aspects of the scene—what seemed to him sculptured madonnas were simply lava blocks resting on top of the tufa cones, a well-known geological phenomenon—but his general description was essentially correct. If anything, it fell short of the fantastic reality.

Taking a close look at what are now but empty shells of a once teeming warren, one still finds much cause for wonder. Some of the earth cones (but only a few) seem so perfect as to have been turned out on a potter's wheel. In a way they look like petrified tepees, except that they sometimes reach the height of a fifteen-story building. The shapes are Nature-made, the result of erosion by wind and water. Cracks and holes dot the surfaces, suggesting some elementary shelter. But perhaps even more than these, the finished silhouette of each peak spells out a *house*. To a man looking for a roof, the rocks were a godsend; he was easily tempted to deepen the natural recesses and cut out, so to say, a niche for himself. Since the porous rock is no more difficult to cut than hardened goat cheese, one man could in no time and without much exertion excavate a good-sized apartment, including some stony furniture: tables, benches, and couches, not to mention fireplaces.

Among the most spectacular of man-made caves are the salt mines (at left and below) of Wieliczka near Cracow, Poland. Staircases and elevators connect seven different levels that reach 800 feet below the ground. The mines have been worked since the eleventh century and now extend over sixty-five miles. Churches that include elaborately carved altars and a ballroom lend the salt mines some upper-world urbaneness.

The fascination of caves has not worn off in our day. On the contrary, the current interest in them, albeit largely orientated toward the decorative kind such as ice and stalactite caverns, parallels the enthusiasm for mountains that swept the world in the eighteenth century, when breaking his neck in the pursuit of alpinism enhanced a man's reputation in much the way dueling did. Today, when mountains have lost their terror and mountain climbing has turned into a sport, cragsmanship takes to tenebrous zones; the trend is from the Olympian to the spelaean. Yet whereas in warm and temperate zones caves have always been valued for their usefulness, the purpose of spelunking is now often no more than an endurance test.

Still and all, and considering that in a country with the appropriate soil it may be cheaper to carve a house out of the ground than to build one—no longer with a whittling knife but perhaps with the help of an attachment to the lawnmower or vacuum cleaner—the question of whether caves ought to be earmarked as general habitations is not as absurd as it may sound. To be sure, the theory that caves might serve as fallout shelters has since been discredited. Nevertheless, if we can read forebodings, a far more awesome prospect than incineration is in store for humanity. To all appearances the time is not far off when our planet will cease to provide as much as standing room for its inhabitants. Even if people were able to adapt themselves to a double- or triple-deck civilization, there is a limit to the rank growth of skyscrapers and multilevel highways. The only way out of the human rabbit warren is, quite simply, down—down the rabbit hole.

Automobiles set the trend long ago. Too bulky and too numerous to find adequate room under the sky, they have taken to tubes and subterranean garages. We may not want to join them immediately. Still, whatever the plans for repairing the damage wrought on the land, chances are that the native genius for destruction will not be daunted by pious vows and mammoth budgets. Free enterprise will prevail. Eventually, though, with nothing left for us to destroy aboveground, we will undoubtedly reassert our proverbial pioneering spirit and depart for

BIBLIOTEKA JAGIELLONSKA, CRACOW

WULF-DIETHER GRAF ZU CASTELL

The square pits in a bleak landscape represent both the most primitive and most advanced concepts of architecture. The Chinese community above is dug into the soft loess, its dwellings grouped around thirty-foot deep courtyards which are entered by L-shaped staircases. Opposite, exemplary of today's good design, are six office buildings which French architect Bernard Zehrfuss recently added to UNESCO *headquarters in Paris. Invisible, indeed unsuspected by passersby, they are a model of discretion—and of an architect's self-denial.*

the virgin territories of a yet unexcavated netherworld.

Yet the experience of all the human and superhuman moles in space and time—the anchorites, gypsies, and trolls of legend—would hardly justify our excursion into the realm of caves were it not that, unsuspected and unknown to us, many millions are today housed underground. So ardently do we cultivate an ignorance of the ways of life in countries whose inhabitants do not share our philosophy, or the lack of it, that few of us have ever heard of the existence of subterranean *cities*. They bear no resemblance to our world of bargain basements and subway stations, but have been planned from scratch as modern metropolises, complete with government offices, factories, schools, hotels, and habitations. Over the past forty years such cities have been built in northern China. (The epithet "northern" is only relative, since the latitude corresponds to that of the Mediterranean.) In the provinces of Shensi, Shansi, Kansu, and Honan more than ten million people, or about the combined

BERNARD RUDOFSKY

population of Austria and Switzerland, live technically as troglodytes although their standards of comfort and hygiene may not differ much from ours.

This architecture, which we shall call deep-dig—in contrast to high-rise—has an honorable tradition. Northern China is loess country, loess being silt transported and deposited by the wind. Its physical properties are similar to those of soft volcanic earth. It ranks lowest in the geological scale of hardness. Rivers saw deeply into its surface, and so do roads by the erosive action of wheels. Roads form the narrowest of canyons, many stories deep and hidden from view.

Loess also happens to be extremely fertile. Hence farmers, unwilling to waste any land by putting houses on it, prefer to make their homes in the bowels of the earth. Staircases and sunken courts for admitting daylight and air are often their only link with the upper world. There may be no houses in sight, but "one may see smoke curling up from the fields," as George B. Cressy writes in his *Land of the 500 Million;* "such land does double duty, with dwellings below and fields upstairs."

A splendid concept, but it seems to have no application for our country. For all we know, agriculture is on the way out here; steadily declining, another victim of progress, it may survive as a hobby at best. But the land gained thereby will come in handy enough. With all architecture safely tucked away below ground, we should be one step nearer to solving the seemingly unsolvable situation of surface traffic. When the entire land will have been asphalted over, making any road system obsolete, cars can move freely in all directions.

As yet we may not be ready for troglodytism. But sooner or later it will become the big issue of national, indeed global, defense—not against the onslaught of foreign nations but against that foe in our midst, the implacable automobile. Our survival will be determined not by abstract ideologies but by the race between the stick-in-the-loess and the builder of castles in the air.

DE MORTUIS

In the business of cheating death, Forest Lawn has a lot to learn

By J. H. PLUMB

The British have hilarious fun over the quaint funerary habits of the Americans. The death of Hubert Eaton, the world's greatest entrepreneur of death, and the recent discovery of a funeral home for pets, by a wandering British journalist, released another gale of satirical laughter in the English press. The mockery was hearty and sustained; yet was it deserved? Well, certainly much of Mr. Eaton's Forest Lawn is hard to take—the wet, nursery language for the hard facts of dying ("the loved one" for the corpse, "leave taking" for burying, and "slumber" for death), the cosmetic treatment (the contortions of death waxed away, replaced by rouge and mascara and fashionably set hair)—all of this is good for a gruesome joke. The place names of Forest Lawn appall—Lullabyland, Babyland. The piped guff, the music that flows like oil, and the coy fig-leaved art give one goose flesh.

One turns, almost with relief, to a harsh fifteenth-century representation of the dance of death—livid corpses, jangling bones, and skulls that haunt. How wholesome, after Hubert Eaton, seem the savage depictions by Bonfigli of the ravages of plague, or even the nightmares of death painted by Hieronymus Bosch. And how salutary in our own age to turn from Forest Lawn to the screaming, dissolving bodies of a Francis Bacon painting, for surely this is how life ends for most of us, in pain, in agony.

WIDE WORLD

Forest Lawn

And if Forest Lawn nauseates, what of the Pets Parlor? "Blackie" combed and brushed, stretched out on the hearth rug before a log fire, waits for his sorrowing owners. The budgerigar is wired to its perch. The Ming Room houses the Siamese cats, and if you want to do your kitty proud, you can spend three hundred dollars or so on a stately laying out, a goodly coffin (if you're worried about its fun in the afterlife, you can put an outsize rubber mouse in with it), and naturally a special plot in Bide-A-Wee, the memorial park for pets. Vice-President Nixon's dog, Checkers, had the treatment: he lies among the immortals in Bide-A-Wee, like Hubert in Forest Lawn.

The dance of death

BIDE-A-WEE PET MEMORIAL PARK

Checkers at Bide-A-Wee

However, this will become a mere second-class death if deep-freezing really catches on, as it shows every sign of doing. The Life Extension Society is spreading, and the entrepreneurs have smelled the profit in immortality. As soon as the breath goes, get yourself encapsulated in liquid nitrogen and stored in one of the specially constructed freezers that are springing up all over America from Phoenix to New York. And so wait for the day when they can cure what you died of, or replace what gave way—the heart, the brain, the liver, or the guts—or rejuvenate your cells.

CRYONICS SOCIETY OF NEW YORK, INC.

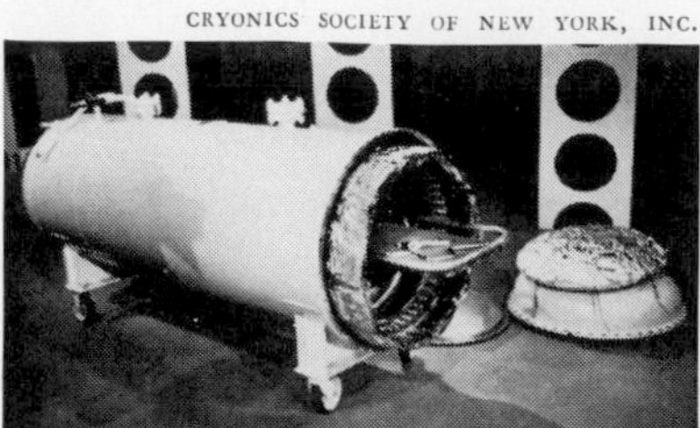

Immortality's deep-freeze

None of this is cheap: the capsule costs four thousand dollars, and then there are the freezing costs and who knows what they may be in fifty years, so it would be imprudent not to make ample provision. Forest Lawn may be death for the rich; this is death for the richer, death for the Big Time. But in America there are a lot of very rich, so maybe soon now, outside all the large cities, there will be refrigerators as huge as pyramids, full of the frozen dead. This surely must be a growth industry.

Perhaps by the year 2000 Hubert Eaton will seem but a modest pioneer of the death industry, for who does not crave to escape oblivion? The rich have always tried to domesticate death, to make death seem like life. The American way of death is not novel: seen in proper historical perspective it reaches back not only down the centuries but down the millenniums, for it is a response to a deep human need.

Some of the earliest graves of men, dating from paleolithic times, contained corpses decked out with bits of personal finery and sprinkled with red ocher, perhaps the symbol of blood and life, done in the hope of a future resurrection. After the neolithic revolution, which created much greater resources and considerable surplus wealth, men went in for death in a very big way. Doubtless the poor were thrown away, burned or exposed or pushed into obscurity, back to the anonymous mind from which they came.

The rich and the powerful, high priests and kings, could not die; they merely passed from one life to another. Because the life hereafter was but a mirror image of life on earth, they took with them everything they needed—jewels, furniture, food, and, of course, servants. In the Royal Graves at Ur, some of the earliest and most sumptuous of tombs ever found, a row of handmaidens had been slaughtered at the burial—death's necessities were life's. No one, of course, carried this elaboration of funerary activity further than the Egyptians. And the tombs of Pharaohs and the high officials of the Egyptian kingdom make Forest Lawn seem like a cheap cemetery for the nation's down-and-outs.

What should we think of vast stone mausoleums outside Washington, stuffed with personal jewelry from Winston's, furniture from Sloane's, glassware by Steuben, food from Le Pavillon, etc., etc., and in the midst of it all the embalmed corpse of a Coolidge or a Dulles? We should roar with laughter. We should regard it as vulgar, ridiculous, absurd. Pushed back three millenniums, such habits acquire not only decorum but also majesty, grandeur, awe.

The Egyptians were as portentous in death as in life, and their grave goods only occasionally give off the breath of life, unlike the Etruscans, who domesticated death more completely and more joyously than any other society. A rich caste of princes built tombs of singular magnificence, filling them with amphorae, jewels, and silver. And they adorned

HARRY BURTON

Egypt's King Tut

their walls with all the gaiety that they had enjoyed alive. There was nothing solemn about their attitude to death. In their tombs they hunted, played games, performed acrobatics, danced, feasted; their amorous dalliance was both wanton and guiltless. Deliberately they banished death with the recollected gusto of life. No society has brought such eroticism, such open and natural behavior, to the

ROBERT EMMETT BRIGHT, RAPHO-GUILLUMETTE

Etruscan tomb

charnel house. But in the annals of death, Etruscans are rare birds.

How different the grandiose tombs of medieval barons, with their splendid alabaster or marble effigies. There they lie, larger than life, grave, portentous, frozen in death, a wife, sometimes two, rigidly posed beside them, and beneath, sorrowing children, kneeling in filial piety, the whole structure made more pompous with heraldic quarterings. Yet these are but another attempt to cheat death, to keep alive in stone what was decaying and crumbling below. And even here a breath of life sometimes creeps in. The Earl and Countess of Arundel lie side by side, dogs beneath the feet, pillows under the head, he in armor, she in her long woolen gown. But, movingly enough, they are holding hands. The sons of Lord Teynham cannot be parted, even in death, with their hawk and hound. Nor were these tombs so cold, so marmoreal, when they were first built. They were painted, the faces as alive with color as the corpses in the parlors of Forest Lawn.

Seen in the context of history, Forest Lawn is neither very vulgar nor very remarkable, and the refrigerators at Phoenix are no more surprising than a pyra-

© A. F. KERSTING

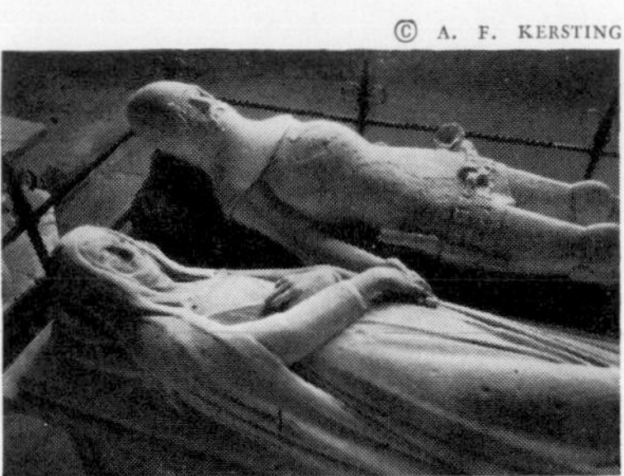

The Arundels at rest

mid in Palenque or Cairo. If life has been good, we, like the rich Etruscans, want it to go on and on and on, or at the very least to be remembered. Only a few civilizations have evaded expensive funerary habits for their illustrious rich, and these usually poverty-stricken ones. For all their austerity, the Hindus, burning bodies and throwing the ashes into the Ganges, have maintained distinction in their pyres. Not only were widows coaxed or thrown onto the flames, but rare and perfumed woods were burned to sweeten the spirit of the rich Brahman as it escaped from its corrupt carapace. Cremation à la Chanel!

What is tasteless and vulgar in one age becomes tender and moving in another. What should we say if we decorated our tombs with scenes from baseball games, cocktail bars, and the circus, or boasted on the side of our coffins of our amatory prowess, as erect and as unashamed in death as in life. And yet when the Etruscans do just these things, we are moved to a sense of delight that the force of life could be so strong that men and women reveled in it in their graves.

So the next time you stroll through Forest Lawn, mildly repelled by its silly sentimentality, think of those Etruscans; you will understand far more easily why seven thousand marriages a year take place in this California graveyard. After all, like those Arundels, Eros and Death have gone hand in hand down the ages. The urge to obliterate death is the urge to extend life, and what more natural than that the rich should expect renewal. How right, how proper, that Checkers should be waiting in Slumberland.

This article by Dr. J. H. Plumb, Horizon's *European Consulting Editor, is the second in his series of comments on contemporary manners in the light of history.*

A Place to Play

Riis Plaza makes the most of the least space

An igloo in a playground? Why not, thought landscape architect Paul Friedberg. So he built one (opposite), connected it with a curved trapeze to a nearby pyramid, and, for good measure, imbedded a slide in its side. And sure enough, it was covered with delighted children even as Mrs. Lyndon B. Johnson was dedicating Riis Plaza in New York. The presence of the President's wife underscored the importance of the imaginative plaza, namely its location (the central mall of a massive low-income housing project in the slums of Manhattan's Lower East Side) and its financing (a $900,000 private grant by the Vincent Astor Foundation). But the real test of the plaza's unique design has been the omnipresence of the children, who scramble from the play-pit, through the central sitting area dotted with concrete sculpture, into the sunken amphitheatre enclosed by a brick-and-timber pergola (below), until they reach the outdoor "room" with the abstract fountain. "We wanted a permissive design that would at once provide a continuous play experience and still meet the needs of all ages," explains Friedberg's collaborator, Simon Breines. His architectural firm, Pomerance and Breines, deliberately used a wide variety of building materials in the multilevel plaza "to emphasize the contrast with the brick, geometric high-rise project houses. In the process, we've discovered that if kids can climb, run over, or jump on something, then they won't break it or deface it. They just enjoy it."

Photographed for Horizon by Ruth Orkin

Families come from all over New York City to enjoy the daytime tranquillity of the Riis amphitheatre (above), which on summer evenings resounds with everything from Shakespearean blank verse to rock-'n'-roll ensembles.

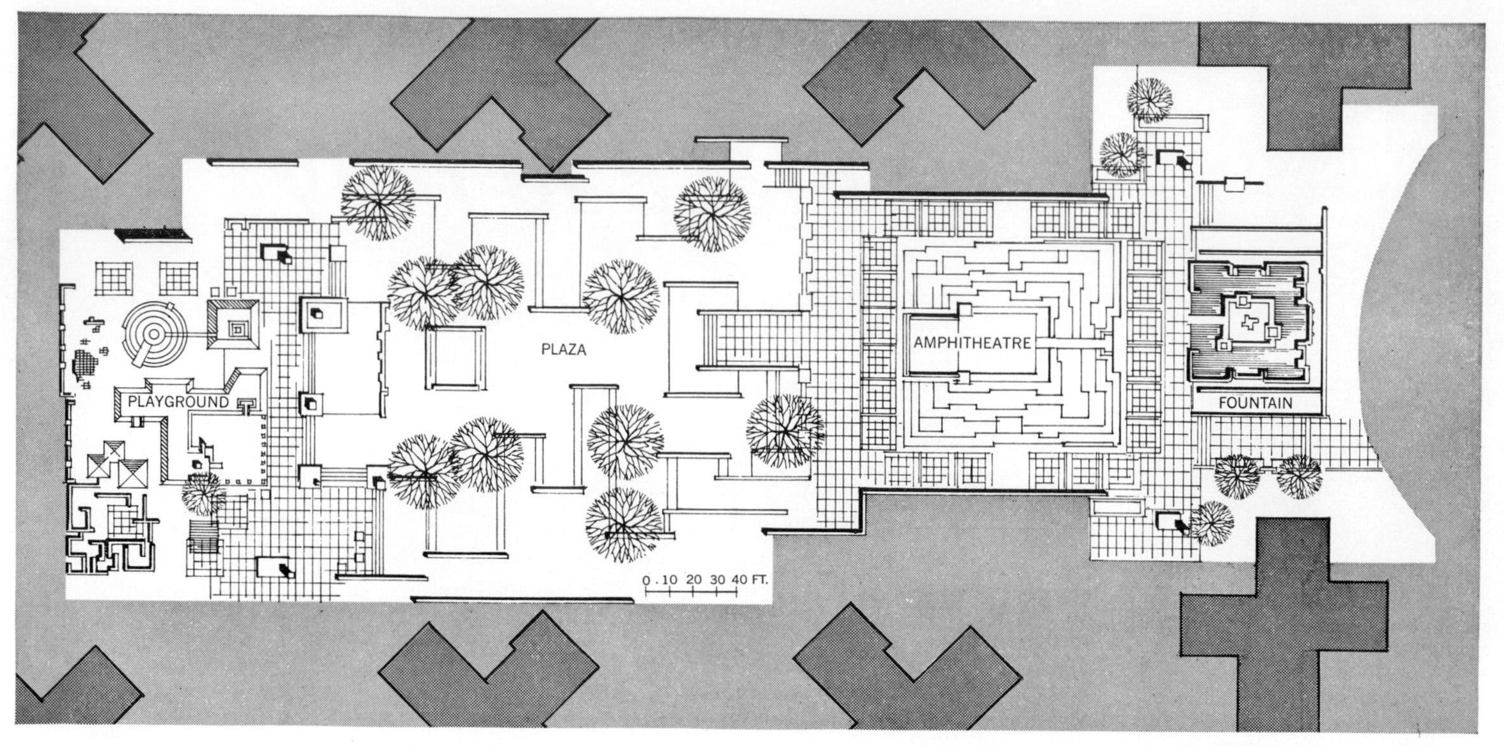
PLAYGROUND
PLAZA
AMPHITHEATRE
FOUNTAIN
0 10 20 30 40 FT.

In redesigning the central mall of the housing project, the architects combined all the social functions into a "continuous living plan." A diagram of Riis Plaza shows, from right to left, the fountain "room," the sunken amphitheatre with its hidden jet sprays for water activities on hot days, the central sitting area (for grownups), and the sand-floored play-pit, which, despite its compactness (see overleaf), offers children all the varieties of play experiences shown on these pages.

LOST: The Trojan War

Almost a full century has passed since Schliemann discovered the site of Troy. Yet no one has found any evidence that the Greeks ever fought there

By M. I. FINLEY

The capture of Troy and the wanderings of Odysseus have had an unrivaled hold on the imagination for more than twenty-five hundred years. The chain of tradition is an unbroken one, through antiquity and the Middle Ages down to our own day, when the word "odyssey" is a common cliché along with "Achilles' heel" or "Trojan horse." As far back as 500 B.C. or earlier, the Etruscans had a predilection for scenes of the Trojan War on the Greek painted pottery which they imported into central Italy. The Romans then went further and linked themselves directly with the Trojans by fashioning a new foundation legend, incompatible with their older myth of Romulus, from whom the city was supposed to have taken its name. Their new hero-founder was Aeneas, one of the Trojan survivors, and it was around him that Virgil wrote the great Roman epic the *Aeneid*. The Roman example later spread, and during the Middle Ages it was commonly believed that English history began with Brute (or Brutus) the Trojan, and that the Franks were descended from Francus, son of Hector.

Our oldest and fullest information about the Trojan War comes from the two poems the *Iliad* and the *Odyssey*, some sixteen and twelve thousand lines in length, respectively, and both attributed to Homer (though modern scholars on the whole believe in two "monumental composers," and place them in the eighth century B.C.). Yet they provide nothing like the whole story. The *Iliad* is devoted to a few weeks in the tenth year of the war, ending not with the fall of the city but with the death of Hector, the greatest of the Trojan warriors. The *Odyssey* narrates the wanderings of Odysseus for ten years after the victory, before he could return to his native Ithaca, a small island off the western coast of Greece. There is a good deal of reminiscing, especially in the latter poem, which helps fill out the account, but there are still many missing pieces. For them we depend on fragmentary material scattered throughout Greek and Roman literature of all kinds, such as the great Athenian tragedies, the works of antiquarians and mythographers, or the Latin poems of Ovid. When we try putting all the scraps together, they add up to too many, and often to contradictions. The mythical imagination did not come to an end with the *Iliad* and *Odyssey* but went on creating new variations and combinations as well as reviving old traditions which Homer failed to include.

Episodes of the Trojan legend such as the concealment of Greek warriors in a wooden horse, shown opposite in the relief from a seventh-century B.C. *vase, were favorite motifs of classical art and literature. But there is nothing, apparently, except the durability of the popular ancient legend to buttress the notion that a real Trojan War ever took place.*

PHOTOGRAPH: GERMAN ARCHAEOLOGICAL INSTITUTE, ATHENS, MYKONOS MUSEUM

Inconsistencies arose even about the most central figures. Everyone was agreed, for example, that Helen was the daughter of Zeus and Leda (wife of King Tyndareus of Sparta), but Homer chose to ignore the most interesting and most famous element in the story of her birth. This is how Euripides has Helen herself tell it (in Richmond Lattimore's translation), at the beginning of his tragedy named after her: "Nor is my own country obscure. It is a place called Sparta, and my father was Tyndareus: though they tell a story about how Zeus

took on himself the shape of a flying swan, with eagle in pursuit, and came on wings to Leda my mother, and so won the act of love by treachery. It may be so."

Helen had twin brothers named Castor and Pollux. In the *Iliad* they are mortals (in fact they are already dead), whereas the later Greeks generally believed them to be gods; they were worshiped in Sparta, among the Greek settlers in southern Italy, and elsewhere. Not later than 550 B.C., furthermore, a lyric poet named Stesichorus introduced a radically new twist designed to save Helen's reputation now that moral values had undergone a change. In this version, Paris got Helen as far as Egypt, and there good King Proteus (the Old Man of the Sea) hid her and replaced her with a ghost, whom the addled young Trojan prince took home with him, deluded into thinking that he had the flesh-and-blood Helen.

Such examples can be multiplied a hundredfold. They did not go unnoticed among educated Greeks, and something of a scholarly literature on the subject developed in antiquity. Thus, the great geographer Eratosthenes (who died in 194 B.C.) dismissed as idle the attempts to identify in Sicily and Italy the places where Odysseus had his wondrous experiences—a game which is still being pursued by some modern scholars. "Homer," he wrote, "neither knew them nor wished to set the wanderings in familiar places." But not one Greek or Roman is on record as having rejected the historical truth of the tale as a whole. Herodotus, the "father of history," a far more penetrating and far less gullible inquirer than he is often made out to be, ascribed the beginnings of mutual hostility between Greeks and Asiatics to the Trojan War, when "the Greeks, for the sake of a single Spartan girl, collected a vast armament, invaded Asia, and destroyed the kingdom of Priam." In the next generation the still more tough-minded Thucydides introduced and justified his history of the war between Athens and Sparta by arguing that it was the greatest war ever, greater even than the Trojan War. The early Church Fathers, too, had to make allowance for Homer, and an entertaining debate arose between pagans and Christians over the question of priority between Homer and Moses.

In brief outline, the tale they all believed was this. Paris, otherwise called Alexander, one of the sons of King Priam of Troy (or Ilion), visited Sparta and fell in love with Helen, wife of King Menelaus. His love was returned, thanks to Aphrodite (whom the Romans called Venus), and the pair fled Sparta for Troy, where they lived more or less happily as man and wife. Menelaus turned for help to his more powerful brother Agamemnon, king of Mycenae. They summoned other Greek princes and chieftains to join in an invasion of Troy, and together they mustered an armada of 1,186 ships in which they set sail from Aulis on the Euripos Strait, between Euboea and the Greek mainland. In the tenth year of the war the Greeks defeated the Trojans and their Asiatic allies; Troy was captured and razed, honor was restored, and some of the returning heroes then entered upon a new series of adventures. While Menelaus and Helen settled down to a peaceful old age in Sparta, Agamemnon was promptly killed by his wife Clytaemnestra (Helen's sister) and her paramour. It was another ten years before the god Poseidon finally allowed Odysseus to see his home again.

The gods played an active part all through the story. But in order to retain the "human" side as actual history, modern scholars have found it necessary to disregard such divine interventions as poetic license or allegory or irrelevant pagan superstition. Nor is this the only difficulty. There is a scene in the *Iliad*, for example, in which Helen stands with King Priam on the ramparts of Troy and identifies some of the main Greek leaders for him, an odd thing to have to do after ten years. In all those years not a single replacement seems to have been sent to the expeditionary forces, nor does much else seem to have been happening at home. Clytaemnestra took a lover, but otherwise time stood still while everyone waited passively for the war to end.

Stripped of the magic of its poetry and its leisurely pace and richness of detail, the Homeric tale sounds flat and not very credible. But then, one could reduce all great events, whether of legend or of history, to the same empty mediocrity, and that is not my intention. It is precisely the Homeric genius which captured the imagination and which therefore is basically responsible for the way poetry became converted into history. Nor was it only the ancients who accepted the account as true in its essentials, despite the gods and the inconsistencies; so did nearly everyone else down to the nineteenth century.

The rise of modern historical criticism at that time led to serious doubts, and then to outright rejection, of the historicity of the Trojan War. The English liberal and banker George Grote, whose twelve-volume *History of Greece*, published between 1846 and 1856, was the first major modern work on the subject (and one of the greatest ever written), had no hesitation in calling the whole Trojan story an "interesting fable." Despite its great appeal, he wrote, "it is a mistake to single it out from the rest as if it rested upon a different and more trustworthy basis."

The view reflected by Grote was rapidly gaining ground until Schliemann turned the tide with his archaeological discoveries. The latter seized on an idea which was being bruited about that the lost city of Troy lay buried within an 85-foot-high mound called Hissarlik, in the northwestern corner of Turkey, about four miles from the Aegean Sea and dominating a large and fertile plain. He began to dig there in 1870 and at once found fortification walls. Soon he produced incontrovertible proof that Hissarlik had been an important citadel with a long history, unearthing, among other things, weapons, jewelry, and gold and silver objects.

Six years later Schliemann turned his attention to Mycenae in Greece, and within a few weeks again struck gold —literally—when he uncovered the so-called Shaft Graves with their remarkable treasures. In his mind that was double proof, material proof, of the Homeric tales; that was the "independent evidence," the lack of which men like Grote had made so much of. In the ensuing decades Schliemann's arguments, supported by further archaeological discoveries, won over just about everyone. It can no longer be seriously doubted that Hissarlik is the Troy of legend and history, even to such details as the masses of horse bones found there. "Thus they performed the funeral rites for Hector, tamer of horses" is the final line of the *Iliad*. Nor can it any longer be doubted that many of the places in Greece (though not all) named in the Homeric poems as the seats of power were in fact important centers in the period when the Trojan War supposedly took place.

However, it is necessary to be equally clear about what archaeology has not substantiated. The Homeric description of the site of Troy is sufficiently unlike the actual site to warrant the verdict of Professor Rhys Carpenter of Bryn Mawr, who wrote in 1946 that "there is something wrong either with Schliemann's Troy or with Homer's." Nor did the mainland Greek coalition (or anyone else) level Troy to the ground once and for all: the site was reoccupied and the ruins rebuilt after each of several destructions. To be sure, these are not decisive objections, and they can legitimately be attributed to the inaccuracies and exaggerations inevitable in the transmission of a tale by word of mouth for many centuries. But the difficulties with the date of the war are more serious. The two great "treasures" that Schliemann found, at Troy and at Mycenae, belong to the wrong civilizations. The war which lay at the core of the tradition could not have occurred at the time when either of the two "treasures" was deposited. The Trojan one falls in the era which archaeologists now call Troy II, 2500–2200 B.C., before there were any Greeks in Europe at all and about a thousand years before the Mycenaean age in Greece. And the Shaft Grave treasure of Mycenae is also too early, being dated before 1500 B.C. The next flourishing period in Trojan history, its mightiest to judge from the fortifications, is Troy VI, which lasted from about 1800 to about 1300 B.C., the period when the horse made its appearance in that part of the world. Troy VI also ended in massive destruction, not only at the wrong time again but, worse still, apparently as the result of earthquake.

Troy VI was immediately followed by a shabby, impoverished community huddled in one small sector of the ridge, as unlike the Homeric picture of the large and wealthy city of Priam as one could imagine. That city, Troy VIIa, was also destroyed, and it—if any—unfortunately has to be the city of the Trojan War. At least it had links with mainland Greece, as shown by the Mycenaean potsherds found by the excavators, and the date of destruction—the guesses range between about 1260 and 1200 B.C.—does fall within the right century, the age of the big palace centers in Greece. Nothing has been found, however—and it is necessary to stress that "nothing" is to be understood literally, not a single scrap—that points to *who* the destroyers were. In other words Trojan archaeology has not been able to substantiate the Homeric tales on this most essential point, despite repeated assertions by archaeologists and historians to the contrary.

What about Mycenaean archaeology, then? Troy has not produced a single written text, in any language, but we can now read the clay tablets, written in a script conventionally called Linear B; they have been found in Mycenae and Pylos in Greece (and a few in Thebes in 1964), as well as at Knossos in Crete. What do they contribute to a solution of the puzzle? The plain answer is that they, too, have not come up with a single scrap of information which points explicitly to Troy or a Trojan War, or even so much as mentions Troy. The best that can be squeezed out of all our new knowledge of this period in Greece is a number of statements beginning "if there really was a Trojan War"—then Mycenae and Pylos and other centers named in the *Iliad* were strong enough in the century from 1300 to 1200 B.C. to assemble a considerable invasion force, and they had contacts with various places on the Turkish coast, and they might have joined in a coalition. But these are all "might have beens" and no more.

Our only ground for thinking that there was a Trojan War remains the old tradition, and the motives for such a complicated overseas expedition still have to be explained. Herodotus may have believed that the abduction of Helen was reason enough, but no serious historian today is prepared to rest his acceptance of the war on such a paltry excuse, romantic though it may be. And no acceptable alternative comes to mind naturally. The pottery reveals continuous trading relations not only with Troy but also with other Levantine regions, and there is nothing to suggest a trade war. If one imagines a raid for booty, the objections are, first, that the war we are told about is wildly out of scale, even allowing for poetic exaggeration; second, that the raiders made a terrible mistake in going after a miserable place like Troy VIIa when there were any number of more profitable possibilities, and that they can be assumed to have known enough about the whole area to have avoided so preposterous an error.

One further source of information needs to be explored. In precisely the two centuries we call the Mycenaean age, the fourteenth and thirteenth, the Hittites controlled a considerable empire, which embraced most of present-day Turkey, made its influence felt in Syria, and dealt on a level of equality with Egypt and Assyria. The royal archives of the Hittites, discovered in 1907 at Boghaz-Köy in central Turkey, include thousands of official documents of the kind that the Linear B tablets of Greece have failed to produce: laws, decrees, and treaties. Perhaps twenty texts, most of them unfortunately in a fragmentary condition, mention a kingdom or territory called Achchijawa, which was independent, usually on more or less friendly terms with the Hittites, but lesser in size and power. Once a sick Hittite king summons the gods of Achchijawa in his search for a cure; another time an enemy is banished to Achchijawa; still another time, when the Hittites are at war with Assyria, the Hittite king orders that "no ship shall sail there from the land of Achchijawa."

The relevance of all this lies in the probability that "Achchijawa" is the Hittite form of the Greek "Achaea." The Homeric poems employ three different names for the Greeks, the most common of which is "Achaeans." If, therefore, the identification Achchijawa-Achaea is correct—the philological argument is complicated and not all experts are satisfied—then the Hittite texts confirm the authenticity of the Homeric tradition on one important point, since "Achaean" ceased to be a generic name for the Greeks in later times.

Again trouble follows at once. Where was Achchijawa located? The Hittite documents offer no satisfactory clues, but imply that Achchijawa, like the other territories mentioned, somehow adjoined Hittite territory. That would exclude the Greek peninsula, though a few historians still try to place Achchijawa there. The island of Rhodes is one plausible suggestion, and there is archaeological evidence of Mycenaean activity on the island in this period. Be that as it may, the great disappointment is that nothing points to Troy. Barring one possible and uninformative exception, Troy is never mentioned, at least not in any recognizable form, in a Hittite document, whether in connection with Achchijawa or in any other context. There is no archaeological evidence of trade or even influence from the Hittites to Troy or vice versa. The Hittite sphere apparently stopped short of the northwestern corner of Turkey. And thus, whatever the truth about Achchijawa, no direct light is shed on Graeco-Trojan relations in general or on the Trojan War in particular. Nor did the Hittites make any impact on the Greek tradition: there is not a trace of them in the Homeric poems or in any of the other bits of the composite legend that have survived.

The documents of the last decades of the thirteenth century reveal that the Hittite empire was in trouble. By 1200 or 1190 it was destroyed. No text tells us who accomplished that, but we now have a pretty good idea of what was going on. By 1200 or 1190 Troy VIIa, too, had fallen; so had most of the great fortresses in Greece and important local states in northern Syria such as Ugarit (modern Ras Shamra) and Alalakh; there was turbulence in the west, in Italy, Sicily, and Libya; there were repercussions as far east as Babylonia and Assyria. All this did not happen at once, but it was concentrated within a few decades. It would be going too far, on present evidence, to suggest a single unified operation, but there is a case for thinking that the main impulse was a massive penetration by migrating invaders from the north, similar in scale, procedure, and effects to the later Germanic migrations into the Roman Empire.

These invaders sometimes appear in modern writings under a misleading name, "Sea Peoples," thanks to a careless reading of two important Egyptian documents. The first records how, about 1220 B.C., Pharaoh Merneptah staved off an attack in the Nile delta by the king of Libya and "Sea People" mercenaries. The second and more important is an account of the successful resistance by Pharaoh Ramses III of a full-scale land and sea invasion through Syria in about 1190. Neither text actually says "Sea Peoples"; they imply that the invaders came from across the sea, and the earlier one is quite specific: "northerners coming from all lands." Various names are listed, but identification is very speculative except for the Peleset of the Ramses engagement, who were surely the Philistines. Presumably they turned north after their defeat and settled on the Palestinian coast, where we find them in the Old Testament period. One of the groups in the 1220 raid is called Akawash, and it is tempting to see Achaeans again, this time lurking behind an Egyptian variant of the name. The difficulty is that the Akawash are described as circumcised, a fact which the Pharaoh mentions on his victory monument because the consequence was to deprive him of his favorite trophy, the foreskins of vanquished enemies. The Greeks, of historical times at least, did not practice circumcision.

The Greek tradition knew nothing about the "Sea Peoples" and the damage they wreaked from Italy to Asia. It did not "remember" the wholesale destruction of the Mycenaean centers, nor even that there had been a Mycenaean civilization which came to an end about 1200 B.C., to be replaced by a new kind of society that was eventually to become their own. For the later Greeks, Agamemnon and Odysseus and Achilles were essentially Greeks like themselves. They were, however, more heroic and at the same time more primitive, and that is why they could be permitted to organize an otherwise incredibly massive expedition "for the sake of a single Spartan girl."

The historical problem we are now presented with is whether the great destructive wave culminating in the eastern Aegean about 1200 or 1190 provides the correct context within which to place and explain the archaeologically proved disaster that befell Troy VIIa at this time. Since an affirmative answer seems plausible, there is nothing to prevent us from going further and suggesting that there may have been Achaean participants. In so greatly disturbed a period it would hardly be surprising if the invading migrants found some friends, allies, and fellow freebooters as they swept through Greece.

But plausibility is not enough. The great majority of scholars still prefer to hold to the tradition, at least to its core. The *Iliad* and *Odyssey*, it is pointed out, are the greatest examples of heroic poetry, a genre known in many parts of the world. Heroic poetry is composed orally, the work of illiterate but highly skilled and professional bards who are able to transmit long and complicated tales from generation to generation. The medieval Grand Prince Vladimir of Kiev was still being sung about in the twentieth century, as was the battle of Kosovo at which the Ottoman Turks administered a shattering defeat to the Serbs in 1389. And the twentieth-century poems contain an element of historical truth on both themes. Therefore, the argument goes, the *Iliad* and *Odyssey*, composed with a genius which the Slavic bards cannot approach, must also have a large historical kernel, and even a much more considerable one.

The Homeric poems have been proved to be right on the name "Achaean" and on the geography of the lost Mycenaean world; by this reasoning they must also be right about the coalition war and the leadership of Agamemnon. Perhaps. But if the Serbian bards could invent tales about the main hero at the battle of Kosovo, and if the French *Song of Roland* can get the enemy wrong, and if the German *Nibelungenlied* can get just about everything wrong; if the Homeric poems contradict most of what we know about the actual working of Mycenaean society, and if their Troy, though in the right place, bears little resemblance to the archaeologists' Troy, and if they are unable to provide a reasonable explanation for the war or a reasonable account of it—then how can one tell what bits, if any, are historical?

In the end, one must return to the genius of the *Iliad* and the *Odyssey*. We no longer read the *Aeneid* or *King Lear* as true stories, as men once did. We certainly do not try to write medieval French history from the *Song of Roland* or medieval German history from the *Nibelungenlied*. Why should we make an exception of Homer's Trojan War?

M. I. Finley, who writes often for HORIZON, *is Reader in Ancient Social and Economic History at Cambridge University.*

ENGLAND, THE MELTING POT

By DAVID LOWE

"He is an Englishman!" proclaimed Sir William Schwenck Gilbert in that most English of English operettas, H. M. S. Pinafore, *and perhaps Gilbert was—though Schwenck has a disturbingly Teutonic ring. But the music which makes the line memorable was the composition of one of the few English composers of the nineteenth century with an international reputation, Sir Arthur Sullivan* **(1)**, *the son of an Irish father and a part Italian mother. And in that we have a clue to the most extraordinary and most overlooked fact of English history. All the best Englishmen have been foreigners.*

The first English saint was Alban of Verulamium **(2)**, who was martyred for his faith at the end of the third century. He was a Roman soldier. When the English next felt the need for a national martyr they were lucky in having at hand Thomas à Becket **(3)**, a Frenchman. Becket, of course, was Archbishop of Canterbury, that prime see of the English church founded in the sixth century by Augustine, an Italian, and whose cathedral, which the English claim as one of their great national monuments, was mostly the work of William of Sens, another Frenchman.

But the English have shown themselves to be as truly catholic in their government as in their church. In that battle upon which all English history appears to swing, Hastings of 1066, the English were led by Harold, whose mother and father were both Danish. As everyone knows, Harold was beaten by William the Conqueror **(4)**—who was a Norman. But then there never has been an English royal house.

When, in the twelfth century, the English grew tired of the Normans, they turned to the Plantagenets, who got their extraordinary name from a shrub favored by Geoffrey, count of the French province of Anjou. Geoffrey's son, Henry II **(5)**, the first of the line to sit on the throne of England, spoke French and laid the foundation of the judicial and administrative system which made English government the model for the world. It was at this time that the legends concerning one of the supreme English literary heroes, King Arthur **(6)**, were gathered together. It should surprise no one that Arthur was a pure Celt. As a matter of fact, the earliest English literary hero, Beowulf **(7)**, was a Swede celebrated in a German epic poem which never mentions England.

Having gone to Denmark, Normandy, and Anjou for their royal house, in the fifteenth century the ever-inventive English went to Wales. There they found the Tudors, whose line was descended from the steward of Llewlyn, prince of North Wales. The first Tudor king, the Welshman Henry VII **(8)**, had the good sense to keep the system of royal councilors which eventually developed into that very English institution, the House of Commons. His son, Henry VIII **(9)**, was one of the fattest men ever to sit on the English throne. We know because of his portrait by the most popular English painter of the period, Hans Holbein, who was German.

In 1605 the main line of the Tudors died out, and in typical fashion, the English went to Scotland, where they found James I **(10)**—he was already James VI of Scotland, thus putting the canny Scots five up on the English. The second Stuart, for that was the name of the new royal house, was Charles I **(11)**, who is remembered because he lost his head and is the only person canonized by the Church of England. Before he lost his head and gained his halo, Charles sported a lovely Vandyck. We know because of his portrait by the most popular English painter of the period, Sir Anthony Van Dyck **(12)**, who was Flemish.

Under Oliver Cromwell's **(13)** Commonwealth (1649–1660) England had the only thing approaching an English monarch in its history, though Cromwell's great-grandfather was one Morgan Williams, and that's about as Welsh a name as you can pronounce. Neither the Irish nor the Scots were happy with an Englishman heading an English government, and they fought long and hard against Cromwell. In time the English themselves grew unhappy with self-government—the Commonwealth is still looked upon as the dreariest period in English history, and the English have had the good sense never to put an Englishman on their throne again. As soon as Cromwell was cold in his temporary grave in Westminster Abbey, the English gave the crown to the son of Charles I and his French queen, Henrietta Maria. Charles II **(14)** had not a drop of English in his purple blood and, as one might expect, he was one of the most popular monarchs in English history.

But after three generations in England the English thought that the Stuarts were behaving too much like natives, and so they drove James II from the throne and offered it to his daughter, Mary **(15)**, who had been sensible enough to live abroad and to pick for her husband William of Orange **(16)**, a Dutchman. Thus, with splendid perversity, the Glorious Revolution of 1688 celebrates the seating of foreigners on the throne of England. Due to a lack of direct heirs and other shenanigans, the English royal house eventually became *Deutsch* rather than Dutch. It was under the second of these German kings from Hanover—they were unimaginative and always named their sons George—that a most English event took place, being not English at all. The most popular piece of English classical music, written by a composer from Lower Saxony under the patronage of an English king who spoke only German, was given a foreign première. The music was *The Messiah* by George Frederick Handel **(17)**, which was first heard in Dublin in April of 1742. The king was George II **(18)**.

The eighteenth century was not only an era of accomplishment for English music, but for English letters and

PICTURE CREDITS: 4: BRITISH MUSEUM; 6: THE METROPOLITAN MUSEUM OF ART, THE CLOISTERS COLL., MUNSEY FUND, 1932; 9: BARON THYSSEN BORNEMISZA, LUGANO; 11: THE METROPOLITAN MUSEUM OF ART, GIFT OF GEORGE A. HEARN, 1906; 12: PRADO—SCALA; 13, 32, 33, 38: NATIONAL PORTRAIT GALLERY, LONDON; 14: VICTORIA & ALBERT MUSEUM, CROWN COPYRIGHT; 17: THE BETTMANN ARCHIVE; 18, 24: COLONIAL WILLIAMSBURG; 21: BRITISH MUSEUM; 25: NATIONAL GALLERY OF ART, WASHINGTON, D.C., ANDREW MELLON COLL.; 26, 28: RADIO TIMES HULTON PICTURE LIBRARY; 29: N.Y. PUB. LIB. PRINTS DIV.; 30, 31: GERNSHEIM COLL., U. OF TEX.; 34: GLASGOW ART GALLERY AND MUSEUM; 35: BROWN BROS.; 39, 40, 44: WIDE WORLD; 41, 43: UPI; 42: WALTER STONEHAM; 45: ROLLIE MCKENNA; 46: ELIOT ELISOFON, *Life* MAGAZINE, © TIME INC.; 47, 48: CAMERA PRESS—PIX

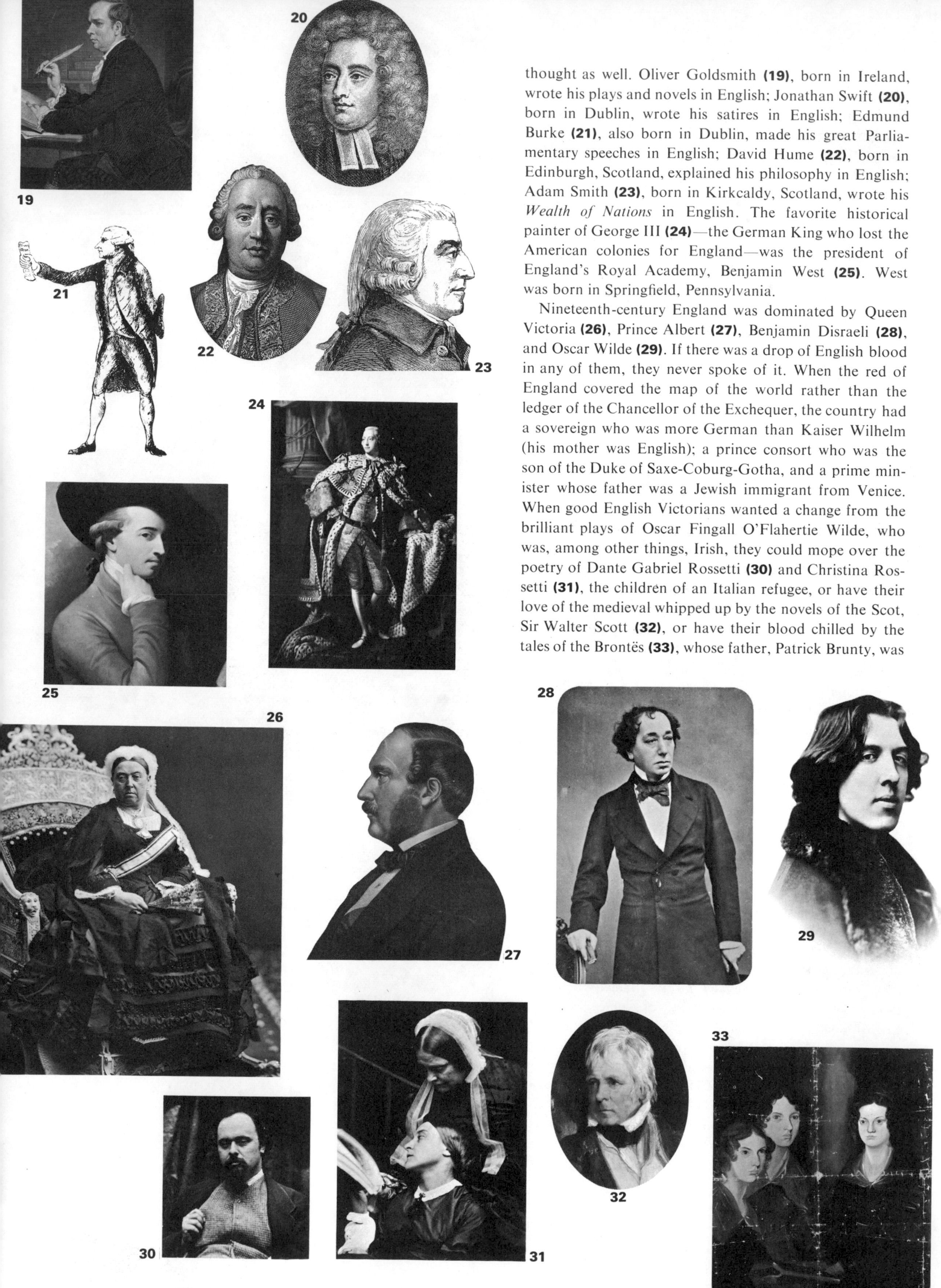

thought as well. Oliver Goldsmith **(19)**, born in Ireland, wrote his plays and novels in English; Jonathan Swift **(20)**, born in Dublin, wrote his satires in English; Edmund Burke **(21)**, also born in Dublin, made his great Parliamentary speeches in English; David Hume **(22)**, born in Edinburgh, Scotland, explained his philosophy in English; Adam Smith **(23)**, born in Kirkcaldy, Scotland, wrote his *Wealth of Nations* in English. The favorite historical painter of George III **(24)**—the German King who lost the American colonies for England—was the president of England's Royal Academy, Benjamin West **(25)**. West was born in Springfield, Pennsylvania.

Nineteenth-century England was dominated by Queen Victoria **(26)**, Prince Albert **(27)**, Benjamin Disraeli **(28)**, and Oscar Wilde **(29)**. If there was a drop of English blood in any of them, they never spoke of it. When the red of England covered the map of the world rather than the ledger of the Chancellor of the Exchequer, the country had a sovereign who was more German than Kaiser Wilhelm (his mother was English); a prince consort who was the son of the Duke of Saxe-Coburg-Gotha, and a prime minister whose father was a Jewish immigrant from Venice. When good English Victorians wanted a change from the brilliant plays of Oscar Fingall O'Flahertie Wilde, who was, among other things, Irish, they could mope over the poetry of Dante Gabriel Rossetti **(30)** and Christina Rossetti **(31)**, the children of an Italian refugee, or have their love of the medieval whipped up by the novels of the Scot, Sir Walter Scott **(32)**, or have their blood chilled by the tales of the Brontës **(33)**, whose father, Patrick Brunty, was from Ireland. If they sought something more demanding in the way of history and philosophy, they could always find it in the books of another Scot, Thomas Carlyle **(34)**. Under these circumstances it is not surprising that when their Parliament buildings burned in 1834, one of the architects the English hired to express their national aspirations in the new edifice was August Charles Pugin, who was French.

During the late nineteenth century, English letters achieved a new glory with the American Henry James, O.M. **(35)**, the Scot Robert Louis Stevenson **(36)**, the Irishman George Bernard Shaw **(37)**, and a novelist born of a Polish family named Korzeniowski, Joseph Conrad **(38)**.

In 1917, after three years of war with the Germans, King George V **(39)**, finally announced that the royal house would henceforth be known, not as Saxe-Coburg-Gotha, but as Windsor. This attempt at Anglicization did not alarm the sensible English, who knew very well that no English blood had tainted the royal family since it had come over from Hanover in the eighteenth century. And so England remained a monarchy while native royal families were being thrown out of their palaces all over Europe. It is true that later on one English king, George VI **(40)**, did marry a lady from the British Isles, the present Queen Mother Elizabeth **(41)**. But at the time he did not expect to become king and, as it fortunately turned out, she was a Scot.

In the First World War the English found their prime minister, David Lloyd-George **(42)**, in Wales; in the Second, they turned to Winston Churchill **(43)**, whose mother, Jennie Jerome (part Iroquois Indian), was from Brooklyn.

During the first half of the present century the most influential Englishwoman was Lady Astor **(44)**, the former Nancy Langhorne of Virginia, who in 1919 became the first female to sit in the House of Commons. The most influential English poet of the period was T. S. Eliot, O.M. **(45)**, of St. Louis, Missouri. Perhaps it was not mere chance that brought the Bishop of Coventry to Sir Jacob Epstein **(46)** when he wanted a sculptor who could sum up the triumph of good over evil for the cathedral he was building to replace the one blitzed by the Nazis. Like Sir Winston's mother, Sir Jacob was from Brooklyn. And it is certainly no surprise that half of those English musical phenomena of today, The Beatles, Paul McCartney **(47)** and John Lennon **(48)**, are Irish. For further reading see the Encyclopedia Britannica, published in Chicago, Illinois.

David Lowe, whose English ancestors were French Huguenots, is a member of the staff of AMERICAN HERITAGE *magazine.*

34 35 36 37 38 39 40 41 42 43 44 45 46 47 48

Many of Lorenz's ideas about human behavior have been provoked by observations of the behavior of the geese he keeps at the Max Planck Institute. Above, he swims with goslings so habituated to his presence that they regard him with the same affection children generally reserve for their mothers.

KONRAD LORENZ

Few men have founded a new science. Lorenz is one who has — the science of ethology, which has a good deal to say about the sources of human aggression

By EDMUND STILLMAN

According to ancient legend, murder came into the world east of Eden when Cain took up a spade and struck down his brother Abel. "And Cain talked with Abel his brother: and it came to pass, when they were in the field, that Cain rose up against Abel his brother, and slew him." All of us know the story, and its meaning. The beast in man, call it original sin, call it id, broke through the barriers of specifically human—*humane*—inhibition and the result was murder.

But now comes a genial Austrian student of animal psychology to tell us the precise reverse. According to Konrad Lorenz, Director of the Max Planck Institute for Physiology of Behavior in Bavaria, the real culprit was the spade! If Cain and Abel, who in the Biblical parable stand for all mankind, had remained what men were in the beginning—more or less weak, slow-moving, vegetarian beasts bereft of fang and claw and incapable of striking down an enemy by a single deadly blow—Abel, like the defeated turtledove, would simply have run away from his angry brother. It was the spade, an artificial weapon, that upset the balance of nature—converting man from a species essentially harmless to itself, to a race of deadly fratricidal killers.

Unlike man, strong, savage beasts of prey such as the lion, the wolf, and the eagle, Lorenz says, very rarely commit fratricide. In a major work, *On Aggression*, recently published in this country, Lorenz declares: ". . . those inhibitions which prevent animals from injuring or even killing fellow members of the species have to be strongest and most reliable . . . in those species which, being hunters of large prey, possess weapons which could easily kill a conspecific. . . . In solitary carnivores, as for example some marten and cat species, it suffices if sexual excitement effects a temporary inhibition of aggression and of preying, lasting long enough to enable the sexes to mate without danger. Large predators, however, which live permanently in a society as wolves or lions do, must possess reliable and permanently effective inhibition mechanisms. These must be sufficiently self-reliant to be independent of the changing moods of the individual. And so we find the strangely moving paradox that the most bloodthirsty predators, particularly the Wolf, called by Dante the *bestia senza pace* [the beast without peace], are among the animals with the most reliable killing inhibitions in the world."

For truly "bestial" cruelty to their fellows, claims Lorenz, we must go to the weak—for it is the weak, in certain circumstances, who murder their own kind. In an early anecdotal work, *King Solomon's Ring*, Lorenz recounts the story of two doves placed in a cage to mate. "Still more harmless than a battle of hares appears the fight between turtle- or ring-doves. The gentle pecking of the frail bill, the light flick of the fragile wing seems, to the uninitiated, more like a caress than an attack." Not so, he warns. Within the feeble heart of the dove a red rage burns. "How could these paragons of love and virtue dream of harming one another? I left them in their cage and went to Vienna. When I returned, the next day, a horrible sight met my eyes. The [male] turtle-dove lay on the floor of the cage; the top of his head and neck, as also the whole length of his back, were not only plucked bare of feathers, but so flayed as to form a single wound dripping with blood. In the middle of this gory surface, like an eagle on his prey, stood the second harbinger of peace. Wearing that dreamy facial expression that so appeals to our sentimental observer, this charming lady pecked mercilessly with her silver bill in the wounds of her prostrated mate."

In the closed quarters of the cage the weaker bird could not flee his implacable mate. The saving mechanism of nature—in this case, flight—had been upset. So with man, Lorenz claims, aggression is an inherent, necessary, and fundamentally *beneficial* motor force. (Indeed, from the transformation of aggression, that "rough and spiny shoot," he argues, paradoxically have bloomed most, if not all, those specifically human institutions of personal friendship and love.) Initially harmless to the survival of our physically weak prehuman ancestors who descended from the trees, aggression within the human species became a demonic force only when the protohuman ancestor first stooped to pick up a stone. With that movement, Cain's symbolic blow of the spade, the harmless beast became a deadly killer—and, as Lorenz says, alluding to the modern German theologians, a "jeopardized creature." Now, ambiguous gifts of nuclear physics and rocket propulsion threaten him and every other species on the globe as well.

The proponent of these and other paradoxical theories regarding the social nature of beast and man is an unassuming yet immensely imposing sixty-three-year-old of rather violently checkered career: boyhood at Altenberg on the Danube in the twilight years of the Hapsburg monarchy, medical studies in New York and Vienna, a professorship in psychology at the University of Königsberg in what was once East Prussia and is now the USSR, military service with the medical corps of the Wehrmacht in World War II, detainment in a Soviet POW camp, and, since then, the friendship of distinguished men like J. B. Priestley and Sir Julian Huxley in England and Erik Erikson in the United States. Today, come to roost at the Max Planck ethological laboratories at Seewiesen, south of Munich, Lorenz directs a staff of some twenty or thirty students and researchers in parklike grounds in the foothills of the Bavarian Alps where the social customs of graylag geese, sheldrakes, Siamese fighting fish, rats, and dogs come under objective scrutiny in natural surroundings. The nerve center of this activity is a large, shabby office that, despite a tank of brilliant coral fish covering an entire wall, somehow gives the impression of an unmade bed. There tame jackdaws and chaffinches flutter about at liberty, perching on a visitor's knee or head. Lorenz himself, unshaven and clad in carpet slippers and faded corduroy trousers, might easily be taken for the janitor.

Lorenz is scrupulous in crediting his predecessors and claims to have "founded" nothing himself; but, together with his close friend and associate Niko Tinbergen of Holland, he is usually credited with establishing the "new" science of ethology; that is, the *comparative* study of the behavior of animals (and men) in their natural surroundings. Ethology is *not* the study of animal psychology pure and simple. Least of all is it the running of rats through an artificial laboratory maze (the standard experiment of American behavioral scientists) or the subjecting of dogs to electrical shocks to determine the mechanism of conditioning so dear to Soviet scientists since Pavlov.

Ethology is an empirical science dedicated to the proposition that the behavior of an organism is as adaptive or unadaptive, and thus subject to the laws of Darwinian natural selection, as are such purely physical characteristics as wing, protective coloration, or speed of foot. Charles Darwin long ago established the principle of *organic* evolution: the inexorable "selection out" of the useless or damaging, and the "selection in" of the useful features that equip the animal in the savage competitive struggle for the means of existence.

Behavior, say the ethologists, like any other natural feature of living beings, is subject to the influences of the two great constructors—mutation, the "accidental" change in the inherited characteristics of an animal or plant, and natural selection. Just as the torpedo shape of such unrelated species as the squid, the mackerel, and the warm-blooded dolphin arose from the common necessity to move fast in water with a minimum of hydrodynamic drag, so are analogous behavior patterns in goose, chimpanzee, and man best understood in terms of the efficiency and survivability of the species. What geese do, say the ethologists, may be a vastly simplified version of what men do, but the analogies are there.

Ethology's theoretical and practical implications for human psychology, sociology, and politics are immediate and profound. Man, says the Bible, is only a little lower than the angels; a contrary, more gloomy view by Shakespeare would have him an angry ape who "plays such fantastic tricks before high heaven as make the angels weep." Neither is quite true, the ethologists say. Man is the most highly organized and adaptable organism to emerge on earth in half a billion years. (Lorenz does not shrink from labeling man a "higher" organism than a squid or a duck, as some schools of self-consciously antiauthoritarian biologists would do.) But man carries a dark burden out of his biological past. On more than one occasion Lorenz, the humanist and provisional optimist, has said that he would weep to think that present-day man is the image of God.

Like his fellow Viennese, Sigmund Freud, whom he admires this side of idolatry, Lorenz believes that man is at best a mixed bag—brilliant and impressive on occasion but, alas, a mixed bag. Not surprisingly, modern ideologues—the theoreticians of such resolutely optimistic philosophies of man as Marxism, and the more implacable environmentalism that still holds sway at Columbia University's Teachers College ("There are no problem children, only problem parents")—react with a most inconsistent aggressiveness to the social implications of Lorenz's work.

Belief in the absolute uniqueness of man dies hard. In the nineteenth century it was chiefly conservative religious opinion that took up the cudgels against Darwin, maintaining the special creation of man by God and of woman from Adam's rib. More insidious was the liberal rejoinder, the passionately asserted faith of nineteenth-century men of good will, like the American anthropologist Lewis Morgan, who seized on evolution—that implacable killing off of the unfit as well as the impersonal triumph of the fit—as new evidence of the goodness of creation. "Democracy in government, brotherhood in society, equality in rights and privileges, and universal education, foreshadow the next higher plane of society to which experience, intelligence, and knowledge are steadily tending," Morgan wrote in 1877, happily oblivious of the approaching carnage of 1914–1945. In this view, nature was man's ally.

More sophisticated in intellectual formulation and, in any event, more cunning in its argumentation has been the assertion of twentieth-century cultural relativists and environmentalists that while the *physical* organism that is man may derive from the ape, in intellectual and characterological terms the gap between anthropoid and humanoid is so wide and so deep as to reduce comparison to absurdity. Man, in this view, is a unique creature of almost infinite plasticity. Ashley Montagu, a typical spokesman for this school, has asserted: "In the course of human evolution the power of instinctual drives has gradually withered away, until man has virtually lost all his instincts," thus dispensing with any dangerously "protoracist" nonsense about the curiously uniform—that is to say, phylogenetically implanted—propensity of infants to laugh or coo with pleasure, and of adults to feel their flesh creep (their body hair bristle) in the dark. "If there remain any residues of instincts in man," Montagu continues, "they are, possibly, the automatic reaction to a sudden loud noise, and in the remaining instance to a sudden withdrawal of support; for the rest, man has no instincts."

The "possibly" is a brilliant forensic touch; but Lorenz, who has seen the horrors of human behavior at firsthand, amid the slaughters of the Hitlerian invasion of Russia, harbors no belief that man is cut off from an animal past. In a curiously terrible and impersonal passage, he has written: ". . . even the simple and seemingly innocuous mechanisms of anonymous flocking can turn into something not only inhuman but truly terrible. In human society, these mechanisms remain more or less hidden, being superseded by nonanonymous, well-organized relationships between individuals, but there is one contingency in which they erupt with the uncontrollable power of a volcano and gain complete mastery over man, causing behavior that can no longer be called human. This horrible recrudescence of the ancient mechanisms of flocking behavior occurs in mass panic. I was once an unwilling witness of the sudden emergence and rapidly snowballing effect of this process of dehumanization, and if I was not drawn into its vortex it was only because, thanks to my knowledge of flocking behavior, I had seen the approaching danger sooner than others and had had time to guard against my own reactions. To me there is small pride in the memory; on the contrary, no one can put much trust in his own self-mastery who has ever seen men more courageous than himself . . . rushing blindly along . . . exactly like stampeding ungulates, and no more accessible to reason than they."

(Lorenz seems reticent on the precise circumstances surrounding the incident, but this, he has confirmed, was at Vitebsk on the Eastern Front during World War II. There a German army seeking to break out of a Russian encirclement made a last desperate effort to break free. Thrown back, all discipline collapsed and order gave way to the animal panic he describes.)

But if man, poor man, carries with him a mixed legacy, both ape and angel, what of Lorenz's main preoccupation, intraspecific aggression—that puzzling habit of widely divergent animal species to fight *within* the biological group, with one another? (In Lorenz's terminology the attitude of cat to mouse, of hawk to sparrow, of marauding Bengal tiger to ox may be appetitive but it is definitely not aggressive—any more than is a businessman's attitude toward the veal cutlet on his luncheon plate. The tiger that stalks the ox hates his intended victim as little as the unsuspecting ox hates the grass on which it feeds.) If animal behavior, like animal morphology, is subject to those iron laws of evolution, mutation and natural selection, if everything in nature demands its explanation, what good can there be in the inherited propensity of the male baboon and the graylag gander to fight, not merely against the predatory lion or fox, but against other male baboons and other ganders? Since these, and the vast majority of other animals that display strong aggression, are social animals, living in groups, does not the incessant warfare mean chaos, reducing the strength of the herd and impairing its ability to fend off attacks from without? If male baboons incessantly fight one another, who will fight the lion?

Lorenz answers that fights within the group are no mere miscarrying of a defensive urge to fight against predators. As Darwin observed long ago, when male baboons fight for females, victory by the strongest ensures that it is the strongest male that passes on his seed. The strength that is tested and selected *within* baboon society ensures that in defense against the lion and the leopard there will be a chance of success. For the extraordinary fact is that when external danger appears male baboons co-operate; the aggression is deflected outward.

But aggression is good for some other things as well. In territorial animals—those that take up a fixed home

—mutual aggressiveness means that competitors will be spread out evenly over an available environment: even within the species there is a fierce competition for shelter and food, since by definition any robin or any stag seeks the same good things in life as any other. Again (and here sentimentalists who would like to see in the "natural" order a precedent for one or another political theory will bridle), social animals tend to organize themselves according to rank. Fights for dominance —to establish the "top dog," to establish the "pecking order"—tend to ensure that the strongest, oldest, and wisest will assert authority in the group, to the general benefit of all.

But of course it is not so simple. All this, Lorenz states, is the function of aggression when evolution works well, but natural selection is not a divine providence; it is not infallible. Working at its best, it merely weeds out those physical and psychological innovations that seriously impair the efficiency of the beast. Natural selection will normally allow any characteristic that is just good enough to survive—not the best, but a shoddy, working B-minus or C-plus of an innovation. And worse still, evolution may miscarry. Before the savage day when a species is, so to speak, called to account, it may produce enormities of grotesque proportions. A frantic competition for mates has led to the enormous spreading tail of the pheasant that so hinders its powers of flight. The vast, unwieldy antlers of the extinct Irish elk were of little avail against the wolf. (Indeed Lorenz believes that on the cultural level the frantic pace of life of Western man is just such a miscarriage of competition within the species. No objective command of nature demands that Western man hurry to his early death by coronary occlusion; but a self-reinforcing system has been built up from which no one, it seems, can break free.)

Competitiveness, or aggression, then, can be lethal when it is uncontrolled or extravagant. Yet aggression is so basic to the mechanism of natural selection that "Nature" simply cannot afford to do without it. A species devoid of all aggression would soon die.

Here, the ethologists maintain, natural selection has hit upon a fruitful compromise. It conserves the aggression as necessary; but in order to avoid total destruction of the group, it governs it, transforms it, or at the very least seeks to deflect it. According to Lorenz, aggression in animals, and man, is in the normal course contained by two processes. The first is simple redirection—against an enemy, another competitive group, perhaps, or toward inanimate objects if need be. The second method, by far the richer in possibilities, is what the ethologists call ritualization. Here, Lorenz claims, man and beast join.

It is in the concept of ritualization that Lorenz and his school are most provocative, for they insist that ritual behavior, designed to control aggression, exists in lower animals. There is, for example, the inflexible custom of the wolf who spares his beaten rival if the impending victim offers his jugular vein. Animal "customs" like these have the closest possible analogies to human morality, say the ethologists.

Viewing a battle for social dominance between two timber wolves, Lorenz records the fate of the vanquished. "The furious whirling of the gray bodies has come to a sudden standstill. Shoulder to shoulder they stand, pressed against each other in a stiff and strained attitude, both heads now facing in the same direction. Both wolves are growling angrily, the elder in a deep bass, the younger in higher tones, suggestive of the fear that underlies his threat. But notice carefully the position of the two opponents; the older wolf has his muzzle close, very close against the neck of the younger, and the latter holds away his head, offering unprotected to his enemy the bend of his neck, the most vulnerable part of his whole body! . . . It now appears that the discomfited fighter proffers intentionally that part of his anatomy to which a bite must assuredly prove fatal. . . . Every second you expect violence and await with bated breath the moment when the winner's teeth will rip the jugular vein of the loser. But your fears are groundless, for it will not happen. . . . A dog or wolf that offers its neck to its adversary in this way will never be bitten seriously. The other growls and grumbles, snaps with his teeth in the empty air and even carries out, without delivering so much as a bite, the movement of shaking something to death in the empty air." But the "victim" is always saved.

Here, Lorenz says, is a functional analogy to human morality: but while human morality is, to some degree at least, conscious and purposeful, the "morality" of the beasts is largely (though in higher animals not wholly) an instinctual gift. Yet in practical terms they are the same, for Lorenz believes that such specifically human institutions as marriage, mercy to the vanquished, child care, and love have arisen, on an instinctual base to be sure, by an analogous process of cultural evolution. Man, having stooped to pick up the stone, has had to evolve, and evolve quickly, reliable inhibitions against smashing in the skulls of all his fellows or, decimated by internecine warfare, the tribe falls prey to the wolf.

Alas for man, the genetically transmitted inhibitions of lower animals function more reliably than our own. But even our own less certain social inhibitions often seem strangely similar in their qualities of slow tempo, stately gesture, inflexible sequence of events, and exaggerated meaning. These qualities enhance *communication*, the certainty of understanding, between two potential foes. Thus for young rebels to question only the *form* of a custom and to ask why the archaic and "useless" husk of ritual cannot be jettisoned and the inner "meaning" retained—achieve religious faith without religious custom, for example—is to miss the point. Social ritual, like genetically transmitted ritual (and in higher animals the line of demarcation between instinct and learned embellishment is not always clear), is an institution in itself. Here form *is* meaning; and once a ritual is established, the desire to act out its forms tends to become, quite apart from "reason" or volition, an appetitive urge of its own.

Ritualization of morals becomes a process whereby the "goal," it might seem, becomes less important than the means. The moral imperatives of inherited law take on a life of their own, and the individual, once made part of the ritual, cannot break free of it without succumbing to anxiety and overwhelming fear.

Lorenz is a vivid and sympathetic observer of the animal world, and the temptation to pile anecdote on anecdote is hard to resist: how graylag geese contract lifelong monogamous marriages (sometimes!) but, if widowed too often, develop a promiscuous tendency and may become the menace of the flock, the *femmes fatales*; how families of rats act like Sicilian bandits, intensely loyal to the clan but murderers to any stranger rat that stumbles their way; how the facial expression of dogs can be exactly correlated to the degree of interaction between the conflicting emotions of aggressive hate and fear.

Intriguing, too, is his allusion to the schooling behavior of minnows, when he relates, "A fish which begins, for any reason, to swim in a certain direction cannot avoid leaving the school and thus finding itself in an isolated position. Here it falls under the influence of all those stimuli calculated to draw it back into the school. . . . the bigger the school and its consequent counterattraction, the less far its members will swim before they return to the school, drawn as by a magnet. A big school of small and closely herded fish thus presents a lamentable picture of indecision. . . . Watching these indecisive actions, one almost begins to lose faith in democracy and to see the advantage of authoritarian politics."

"However," continues Lorenz, "it can be shown by a very simple experiment how little justified this standpoint is. Erich von Holst removed, from a common minnow, the forebrain, which, in this species, is the site of all shoaling reactions. The pithed minnow sees, eats, and swims like a normal fish, its only aberrant behavior property being that it does not mind if it leaves the shoal unaccompanied by other fishes. It lacks the hesitancy of the normal fish, which, even when it very much wants to swim in a certain direction, turns around after its first movements to look at its shoalmates, and lets itself be influenced according to whether any others follow it or not. This did not matter to the brainless fish: if it saw food, or had any other reason for doing so, it swam resolutely in a certain direction and—the whole shoal followed it. By virtue of its deficiency, the brainless animal had become the dictator!"

But here the nagging question comes again—can it all really mean what he says it does? In what true sense is a democracy like a school of minnows? Are democracy's actions as wholly without rationale and purpose as the indecisive searchings of a minnow shoal? Is a dictator really a "pithed" human being, dangerous merely because he is devoid of sympathetic ties to his fellows?

Or is Lorenz wholly serious when he recounts for us the glory of the indecisive minnow shoal and of Ada the promiscuous goose? Is it not, at some level, all deliciously close to a modern version of the charming beast fables of Aesop and La Fontaine? Are we right to ask more?

Unfortunately, the dividing line between the charming Viennese raconteur and the committed man of science is not always easy to define. But Lorenz, at least, is diffident about making political and social deductions from the scientifically observed manner of the beast. Others are not so cautious, so aware of the great and indisputable gap between anthropoid ape, our nearest relative, and sapient, if imperfect, man. Already the American public's curiosity and credulity have been strained by Robert Ardrey. In a book entitled *The Territorial Imperative*, Ardrey has informed us that man, by biological inheritance, is a capitalist: that the failure of Soviet agriculture—the manifest failure, be it said—is the penalty of going against the instinctual territorial proclivities of the human beast. If this is to be the popular result of Lorenz's endeavors, what will have happened is that Lorenz, taking up arms against one school of "theological" biologists, will have given heart to another.

For all his originality of vision, even Lorenz's social analogies often seem forced. Granting the rich possibilities that lie in the concept of ritualization, there is no comparison possible as yet between the sketchy insights given us by the ethologists into the dynamics of ritualization and the Freudians' painstaking working out of the mechanics of libidinal drives.

Human motivation, for all the study, so far remains obscure, not because man is a special creature of providence, but because man is so complex. To solve the interaction of sexual urges and aggression in the graylag gander is one thing. To do so for that "jeopardized creature," man, is quite another—if only because in human beings the expansion, the complexities, and the expansive mechanisms of Lorenz's own act of ritualization have become so immense.

Nonetheless, psychologists, psychiatrists, theologians, and power politicians alike will need to come to terms with his insights, even though his insights cannot, at our present state of knowledge, be taken at face value. He has charmingly told the legend of King Solomon, whose magic ring gave him the power to speak the language "of beasts, and of fowl, and of creeping things, and of fishes." It is a brave beginning—but the ring has not yet quite taught us to speak the language of men.

Edmund Stillman is a historian and an Associate of the Hudson Institute. His most recent book, written with William Pfaff, is Power and Impotence, the Failure of America's Foreign Policy, *published in 1966 by Random House, Inc.*

"Graylag goslings," Lorenz has written, "unquestioningly accept the first living being whom they meet as their mother. . . ." Opposite, Lorenz leads his brood to dinner.

Crusoe's Island

It was actually Alexander Selkirk's.
But in his universal masterpiece
of a man alone, Defoe made it his own

The massif of Juan Fernández Island juts out of the sea as ominously today as it did in 1704, when a rebellious sailor named Alexander Selkirk was abandoned there. His literary descendant, Crusoe, is depicted above just after his shipwreck near the desolate rock. "I clambered up the Clifts of the Shore, and sat me down upon the Grass, free from Danger, and quite out of the Reach of the Water."

About four hundred miles off the western coast of Chile lies the island of Juan Fernández, now called Más a Tierra, where Alexander Selkirk was marooned for four years. The life and adventures of this unruly sailor would by now have been forgotten had it not been for Daniel Defoe, who transformed them into *The Life and Strange Surprising Adventures of Robinson Crusoe,* a tale that cuts across all limitations of age, taste, and social condition and appeals to every man's will to survive.

In the hands of a modern novelist Crusoe's island might have been the stage for a bleak, existentialist drama, but for Defoe it was just the place to show off his hero's virtue, industry, and resourcefulness. Robinson's fate is tempered by the booty he rescues from his foundered ship (a dog, a set of carpenter's tools, a small pot of ink, a seemingly bottomless supply of rum), by the natural advantages of his island (wild game, fresh fruit for the picking, plentiful wood and water), and most of all by his optimistic Protestant temperament. He soon takes up his Bible and learns to marvel at God's mysterious ways, comforting his dark moments with the reflection that he might be worse off than he is. A Defoe of our time would almost certainly represent his Crusoe reverting to savagery, like the castaways in *Lord of the Flies;* but the eighteenth-century Crusoe, safe from modern psychological enlightenment, retains his identity as a civilized Englishman, toils to supply his wants, and takes his pleasure in seeing "all my Goods in such Order and especially to find my Stock of all Necessaries so great." Terror and loneliness exist for him, but he prevails, and so has his improbable but supremely credible story.

Recently, the photographer Sergio Larrain returned to the island and found it much the same as it was in Selkirk's days—despite the addition of a small fishing village. On these pages Mr. Larrain's photographs of the setting of the novel are accompanied by scenes of the events themselves, as shown in engravings taken from nineteenth-century editions of Defoe's work. Peter Quennell, co-editor of *History Today* and a frequent contributor to Horizon, has provided the essay on Selkirk and Crusoe that begins on the following page.

By PETER QUENNELL

The Selcraigs were one of those families who thrive in an atmosphere of strife and discord. They scandalized their Scottish neighbors; they defied authority; with even greater enthusiasm, they wrangled and fought among themselves. Pitched battles were apt to occur upon the smallest provocation. Late in the year 1701, for instance, Andrew Selcraig having carried home a "can full of salt water," his brother Alexander "did take a drink through mistake" and, when Andrew laughed at the face he pulled, Alexander began to beat him; whereupon Andrew rushed out of the house to fetch an elder brother John, while their determined father squatted with his back to the door, meaning, he afterward explained, to prevent Alexander from going "to get down his pistol." John's wife, Margaret, then joined in, assaulted "the said Alexander," who was grappling with both his father and her husband, and, before she was finally bundled into the street, denounced him as a "false loon."

This domestic hubbub attracted the attention of the Kirk elders; and on November 30 Alexander Selcraig, "according to the session's appointment, appeared before the pulpit, and made acknowledgment of his sin . . ." It was not his first offense. Six years earlier, at the age of nineteen, he had received a public rebuke "for his undecent behaviour in the church." But by now he had evidently had enough of his father and the noisy Selcraig household; and sometime in 1702 he said good-bye to Largo, the small Scottish seaport where the elder Selcraig carried on his business as a shoemaker and tanner, and enlisted under an English sea captain who was manning an expedition to the South Seas. Alexander Selcraig, presently renamed Selkirk, must already have served his apprenticeship at sea, though exactly how and where we cannot tell. For, when he enlisted under Captain William Dampier, the renowned ex-pirate and circumnavigator of the globe, he was appointed sailing master of the galley *Cinque Ports*, a vessel of one hundred and twenty tons which was to accompany the *St. George*, commanded by Captain Dampier himself.

SERGIO LARRAIN—MAGNUM

Alexander Selkirk, in bronze, gazes out over the Scottish village of Largo, where he spent his rowdy boyhood. The villagers erected this statue to his memory in 1885.

Thus Selkirk exchanged the squalid confusion of his life at home for the anarchic rigors of a life at sea. The white-winged sailing ship is an imaginative symbol of freedom; during the days of sail, it was more often an inferno of misery and discontent. Below decks there was scarcely room to turn; the food was abominable, and after a long diet of salt-beef and biscuit, men began to rot with scurvy. On ships of the line, savage physical punishments helped to maintain law and order. The ship on which Selkirk had embarked was a petty privateer, one of those vessels which, in times of war, were fitted out to act as licensed pirates, encouraged to harry French and Spanish craft and now and then take by surprise and plunder an ill-defended Spanish settlement.

Dampier's expedition was somewhat unsuccessful, and soon his men were grumbling and his officers were quarrelling. Naturally Selkirk was a major disputant. Early in 1704 the *Cinque Ports* reached the island of Juan Fernández, or Más a Tierra, a stark mountainous volcanic ridge, more than ten miles long and nearly four miles broad, lying about four hundred miles off what is now the coast of Chile. There, Selkirk and forty-one other men announced that they would no longer serve under their incompetent captain, Thomas Stradling, and Selkirk led them ashore, where they organized a kind of sit-down strike. It took all Dampier's powers of persuasion to get them back again. But the expedition continued to go badly, and in May, 1704, the *St. George* and the *Cinque Ports* decided to take different courses.

That autumn the roving *Cinque Ports* returned to the shelter of Juan Fernández. The captain and the sailing master were still at odds. Stradling, his subordinate claimed, was a bungler who did not know his trade; and when the Captain proposed to set sail, Selkirk refused to accompany him and insisted that he and everything he owned should at once be put ashore. This was a serious error of judgment; none of his companions followed. It is said that Selkirk lost heart, tried to rejoin the party, and splashed out after them across the shallows. But he was too late; and he stood there alone, knee-deep in the swirling surf. He shouted after his faithless friends; he expostulated, implored, and argued. The ship's boat gradually drew away; behind him rose the dense green thickets and steep gray precipices of a wild unpeopled island. As the *Cinque Ports* hoisted her sails, he dropped headlong into a deep, appalling solitude.

Loneliness is a theme that has always fascinated the literary imagination. Man is born alone and dies alone; he lives alone amid his secret thoughts and feelings. Selkirk's plight typifies the human condition at its most defenseless and its most unfriended. He was a man thrown back on his own resources, Shakespeare's "poor forked animal" stripped of the armor of civilized existence with which we enclose the naked human organism. He had rejected authority, challenged society; now he had to face himself.

His first reaction was one of passionate despair, accompanied by a thrilling sense of terror. He did not sleep until exhaustion closed his eyes, and seldom ate "till Hunger constrain'd him, partly for grief, and partly for want of Bread and Salt." In his solitude he remembered his childhood training; the riotous young man, whose "undecent behaviour" had so offended the elders of the Kirk, thumbed through his family Bible, prayed aloud, and sang psalms. Then, little by little, the natural man prevailed; he was strong, resourceful, and resilient. His island was no barren rock: "the broken craggy precipices which had appeared so unpromising at a distance," wrote Commander George Anson, an Englishman who visited the island in 1741, "were covered with woods, and between them were interspersed the finest vallies clothed with most beautiful verdure, watered with numerous streams and cascades of clear water." He had his musket with him and a bag of gunpowder, "a Hatchet, a Knife, a Kettle . . . some practical Pieces, and his Mathematical Instruments and Books." Before long he had built "two Hutts with Piemento Trees, cover'd them with long Grass, and lin'd them with the Skins of Goats, which he kill'd with his Gun as he wanted . . ."

When his powder eventually ran out, he learned to chase the goats on foot. Scottish children of his class and period very seldom wore shoes, and Selkirk became a barefooted hunter, capable of outdistancing most of the animals he chased. Juan Fernández at the time abounded in goats which, together with cats and rats, had been established there by previous colonists. The rats were troublesome; they gnawed his horny soles and chewed holes in his precious garments. In order "to defend him against

SERGIO LARRAIN—MAGNUM

Mementos of Selkirk's stay on Juan Fernández, the goblet and two flintlock pistols that he used on the island, are preserved above in the Edinburgh Historical Museum.

them he fed and tamed Numbers of young Kitlings, who lay about his Bed, and preserved him from the Enemy."

Even the "Monsters of the Deep"—seals and elephant seals—whose "dreadful Howlings . . . seemed too terrible to be made for human Ears," ceased to alarm him as he lay awake at night. He dared to approach the slow and stolid creatures, and presently discovered how to kill them "with greatest Ease imaginable." He also caught turtles and crayfish, and plucked the fruit of the pimento trees (thought to have been sandalwood, which has now completely vanished from the island), the leaves of an edible palm, which he called the cabbage tree, and the excellent English turnips that Captain Dampier's crew had planted. The pimento trees, also provided stores of fragrant firewood. Surrounded by some hundreds of amiable cats and a troop of domesticated kids, he led a sober, patriarchal life. Frequently he would sing and dance among his purring, capering household: "so that by the Care of Providence and Vigour of his Youth, being now but about thirty years old, he came at last to conquer all the Inconveniences of his Solitude . . ."

His worst adventure occurred when, pursuing a goat, he fell over an unsuspected precipice and lay stunned and wounded a day and a night, the body of the dead goat awkwardly doubled up beside him. But once more he rallied; he managed to deal with his bodily hurts and ills as efficiently as he had cured his spiritual disorders, and even made good use of a native "black Pepper call'd *Malagita*, which was very good to expel Wind, and against Griping of the Guts."

Yet the longing for human company persisted—almost any company but that of Spaniards, for the War of the Spanish Succession had been raging since 1701. Several ships passed the island like ghosts, "but only two came in to anchor." When Selkirk ran down from his lookout, he recognized a Spanish landing party and had to retreat into the recesses of the island; upon which they fired their guns and gave chase. Once he climbed to the topmost branches of a tree, "at the foot of which they made water, and kill'd several Goats just by, but went off again without discovering him."

At last deliverance came. Toward the end of January, 1709, when Selkirk's solitary reign had lasted four years and four months, a couple of English privateers, the *Duke* and the *Duchess*, commanded by Captain Woodes Rogers with William Dampier aboard as pilot, approached the rocky shores of Juan Fernández. They were alarmed by a distant mysterious light, and although they were eager to leave their vessels—many of the crew were suffering from scurvy—not until the second of February were they resolute enough to send "our Yall ashore." Their alarm soon proved groundless; "all this stir and apprehension arose, as we afterwards found, for one poor naked Man . . ." Not that Selkirk was literally naked; he still possessed a single shirt, and was otherwise warmly clad in goatskins. Nor was his condition really pitiable. Although "at first coming on board us, he had so much forgot his Language for want of Use, that we could scarce understand him," he was sound in mind and body. "Exercise of walking and running" had long ago "clear'd him of all gross Humours." Like most eighteenth-century seamen, Selkirk must have been a

SERGIO LARRAIN—MAGNUM

The sea chest above once held the few possessions with which Selkirk was set ashore and abandoned by the captain of his ship. The bronze tablet on the opposite page was set into the rocks of Selkirk's island some one hundred and sixty years after his sojourn there. It stands near the lookout point where Selkirk spent many hours scanning the lonely seas for a rescuer.

IN MEMORY OF
ALEXANDER SELKIRK,
MARINER,
A NATIVE OF LARGO, IN THE COUNTY OF
FIFE, SCOTLAND,
WHO LIVED ON THIS ISLAND IN COM
PLETE SOLITUDE, FOR FOUR YEARS
AND FOUR MONTHS.
HE WAS LANDED FROM THE CINQUE
PORTS GALLEY, 96 TONS, 16 GUNS, A.D.
1704, AND WAS TAKEN OFF IN THE
DUKE, PRIVATEER, 12TH FEB, 1709.
HE DIED LIEUTENANT OF H.M.S. WEY
MOUTH, A.D. 1723, AGED 47 YEARS.
THIS TABLET IS ERECTED
NEAR SELKIRK'S LOOKOUT, BY
COMMODORE POWELL AND THE
OFFICERS OF H.M.S. TOPAZE, A.D. 1868.

CONZETT & HUBER, ZURICH

Selkirk had no companions on his island, but Defoe provided one for Crusoe. Above, he receives obeisance from Friday

hard drinker, but on this occasion, when "we offer'd him a Dram . . . he would not touch it . . . and 'twas some time before he could relish our victuals."

Selkirk's subsequent adventures were comparatively commonplace. On the voyage home he helped to attack and plunder the Spanish settlement of Guyaquil, in Peru, and he returned to England having accumulated some £800 in prize money. Once he had reverted to so-called civilized life, he underwent a gradual change. Richard Steele, who interviewed him in 1713, reported that when they first met, "there was a strong but cheerful seriousness in his look, and a certain disregard to the ordinary things about him, as if he had been sunk in thought"; but after only a few months, "I could not recollect that I had seen him; familiar discourse in this town had taken off the loneliness of his aspect, and quite altered the air of his face." His violent temper again declared itself; at Bristol, in 1713, he was charged with assaulting one "Richard Nettle, shipwright." He would also appear to have become an unscrupulous philanderer; in 1716 he carried off to London a Scottish farmer's daughter named Sophia Bruce and, she claimed, made her his legal wife. But almost at once he joined the Royal Navy, and then, during a spell of shore leave, in December, 1720, he married a widow, Frances Candish, or Candis, who kept a public house near Plymouth. In 1721 Selkirk died at sea, struck down by a deadly tropical fever.

Meanwhile he had enjoyed his moment of fame. Woodes Rogers's story of his travels, *A Cruising Voyage round the World*, which included the fullest account of Selkirk's experiences, was originally published in the year 1712; and in December of 1713 Steele wrote up his interview with Selkirk as a literary essay for *The Englishman*. Steele was a practiced journalist and a shrewd contemporary moralist. He described Selkirk's struggle against dark and self-destructive impulses, explained how he had conquered his dejection "by the Force of Reason, and frequent reading of the Scriptures," painted the idyllic life he had led once his fears and miseries had been thrust behind him, and concluded by declaring that "this plain Man's Story is a memorable Example, that he is happiest who confines his Wants to natural Necessities" and never seeks to go beyond them. The way was now open for Daniel Defoe, whose *Life and Strange Surprising Adventures of Robinson Crusoe of York, Mariner* reached the world in 1719.

It seems unlikely that Defoe had met Selkirk; and, for his imaginative record of travel, Rogers and Steele were not his only sources. In Dampier's *Voyages* he had read of the Indian castaway, Will, who at the end of the seventeenth century had passed two lonely years on Selkirk's island; and he may also have consulted a recent English translation of an extremely curious Arabic volume, *The Improvement of Human Reason exhibited in the Life of Ebn Yokdan*,* a Muslim castaway who overcomes his surroundings and in solitude obtains an intuitive knowledge of God. Daniel Defoe was an experienced salesman of his work, and travelers' tales were particularly popular at the beginning of the eighteenth century. He was anxious to produce a book that would sell; as a theorist and an artist, he was also keenly excited by the subject of Richard Steele's essay. Selkirk had conquered "by force of reason"; throughout his life Defoe, too, endeavored to apply

SERGIO LARRAIN—MAGNUM; OVERLEAF: SAME

CONZETT & HUBER, ZURICH

The cave at the top is supposed to have been one of Selkirk's refuges. Crusoe, as the engraving above shows, considerably improved such rude accommodations, adding a table and chairs he had hewed out of logs, pots and pans, a homemade basket, and a loving animal family.

OVERLEAF: *To get a lookout point, Selkirk—and Crusoe—had to climb the island's rocky cliffs. The ladder belongs to some modern fisherman, but it is virtually identical to the one that Crusoe fashioned for his own use.*

* See *The Real Robinson Crusoe* by R. L. Mégroz (1939), a study of Selkirk which is particularly interesting on the subject of his early life.

reason—sound, practical, middle-class common sense—to a large variety of current problems.

Thus the island he described became the microcosm of an island commonwealth. Nature had stocked it for the use of Man. How should Man employ those riches, hampered, as he so often was, by the bonds of ignorance and fear and greed? *Robinson Crusoe* is a picture of Reason triumphant; such is the story's universal aspect. On another plane Defoe, who had dabbled in a scheme for colonizing the South Seas, was deeply interested in the problems of modern colonial expansion, and Crusoe's island is the pattern for a colony close to the shores of the South American continent, a region toward which English merchants and "projectors" were then turning greedy, speculative eyes. Defoe's book shows a middle-class Englishman—just such an Englishman as he was himself—in the role of imperial colonist and benevolent administrator.

Robinson Crusoe, the author's first novel, was written and published in 1719, when he was almost sixty. By that year Defoe is thought to have fathered more than two hundred and ninety printed works, none of them downright fiction but covering an enormous range of subjects. His career, like Crusoe's, had been varied: he had dealt in stockings, manufactured bricks and tiles, traveled up and down the country in search of political and commercial information, produced pamphlets on behalf of the Tory government, and more recently, after the Tories had fallen, had undertaken to support the Whigs by posing as a Tory journalist and in that role doing his best to "disable and enervate" the publications of High Tory writers. Once he had been imprisoned and pilloried, but, owing to his clever conduct of the situation, had been pelted with flowers instead of filth and stones.

Meanwhile Defoe had continued to float and abandon endless schemes of self-enrichment, including a scheme to make a corner in civet, the basic material used by the manufacturers of scent. When it failed, he was left with a breeding stock of seventy unwanted civet cats. He had married an heiress, but in 1692 had gone bankrupt, with debts amounting to £17,000, in those days a very considerable sum. During the process he had begotten eight children, whose future caused him grave disquiet; and he was now living among his family in a large old-fashioned house at Stoke Newington. His debts, however, still disturbed him, and he often found it expedient to retire into secret London lodgings.

Few writers have been more extraordinarily industrious; for Defoe, to draw breath was to write and publish, and *Robinson Crusoe,* once he had set his hand to it, seems to have been composed at breakneck speed. The year 1719 was his *annus mirabilis.* It was then that he emerged as a master of the modern art of storytelling. His novel achieved an immediate success, but he did not rest upon his laurels. In 1720, besides continuing *Robinson Crusoe,* whose *Serious Reflections* were now given to the public as a sequel, he published *Life and Adventures of Mr. Duncan Campbell* and *Captain Singleton*; in 1722, the immortal *Moll Flanders, A Journal of the Plague Year,* and *Colonel Jack;* in 1724, *The Fortunate Mistress.* All these books had admirable qualities, but from the point of view of the common reader, *Robinson Crusoe* remains the novelist's unchallenged masterpiece. Its fame spread

SERGIO LARRAIN—MAGNUM; OVERLEAF: SAME

A footprint in the sand (those shown opposite are on the beach at Juan Fernández) so alarmed Crusoe that he fled to his cave for three days and nights. At first he imagined that the Devil had visited him, but he soon concluded "that it must be some more dangerous Creature." The engraving above shows him coming across the terrifying evidence.

CONZETT & HUBER, ZURICH

This vignette shows Crusoe exploring his island under the shade of a parasol. On one of his walks he discovered the wooded side of the island, shown overleaf. ". . . in this Part I found . . . Melons upon the Ground in great Abundance, and Grapes upon the Trees; the Vines had spread indeed over the Trees."

Crusoe learns to his dismay that the mystifying footprint has been left by one of a tribe of cannibals who frequently return to dine upon their captives. After observing these capers through his spyglass (above), he resolves to try to escape, and once he has Friday to assist him, he builds a boat and fits it with a sail and provisions (below).

through the whole of Europe. Even the captious Jean-Jacques Rousseau was to recommend it in *Emile* as the best of educational textbooks.

Yet the world-wide celebrity of *Robinson Crusoe* rests upon a single episode, which, in the nineteenth-century edition before me, occupies only 244 out of 607 pages. Though Crusoe's intrepid voyages through the wilds of China and Siberia are almost as exciting and well described, no one pays much heed to them. It is the island story that holds our attention. The island, like the sailing ship, is a powerfully poetic image which symbolizes both freedom and loneliness, for on an island Man is at once the undisputed master of his surroundings and the isolated victim of his own destiny. The story delights children as much as it interests the adult critic: Defoe appeals to the child in man and to the adult who lies hidden in the child. Every child has built huts and bonfires, has pretended to beat off a host of savages, and has reigned supreme over a troop of friendly animals. But the imaginative child is also naturally creative, and *Robinson Crusoe* is the description of a man planning and creating an entire new world. He is not only the original exponent of self-help, the type of proud suburban householder who embellishes his kitchen or constructs a garden shed; he is the artist, too, and finds the act of creation deeply absorbing and uplifting. Take Crusoe's famous account of how he manages to fire an earthen vessel:

I had no Notion of a Kiln, such as the Potters burn in . . . but I plac'd three large Pipkins, and two or three Pots in a Pile one upon another, and plac'd my Fire-wood all round it with a great Heap of Embers under them; I ply'd the Fire with fresh Fuel . . . till I saw the Pots in the inside red hot quite thro', and observ'd that they did not crack at all. . . . so I slack'd my Fire gradually, till the Pots began to abate of the red Colour, and watching them all Night, that I might not let the Fire abate too fast, in the Morning I had three very good, I will not say handsome, Pipkins; and two other Earthern Pots, as hard burnt as cou'd be desir'd. . . . No Joy at a Thing of so mean a Nature was ever equal to mine, when I found I had made an Earthern Pot that would bear the Fire; and I had hardly Patience to stay till they were cold, before I set one upon the Fire again . . . to boil me some Meat, which it did admirably well.

Defoe's method of writing is as plain and practical as Crusoe's method of furnishing his house. Both are plain men. Although Crusoe wanders around the globe—just as Defoe had explored modern England, from Newgate Gaol to the statesman's cabinet and the anterooms of the British Court itself—in the end, after "a life of infinite variety," he reverts to the sober middle-class station, the "middle state" that, when he was still young and restless, his ancient father had so often praised:

He ask'd me what Reasons more than a meer wand'ring Inclination I had for leaving my Father's House and my native Country . . . He told me it was for Men of desperate Fortunes on one Hand, or of aspiring, superior Fortunes on the other . . . to rise by Enterprize, and make themselves famous in Undertakings of a Nature out of the common Road; that these things were all either too far above me, or too far below me; that mine was the middle State, or what might be called the upper Station of *Low Life*, which he had found

SERGIO LARRAIN—MAGNUM; LEFT: SAME

The highest point of Juan Fernández Island is a towering rock called "El Yunque" (the cloud), because it is usually covered in mists.

by long Experience was the best State in the World . . . not exposed to the Miseries and Hardships, the Labour and Sufferings of the mechanick Part of Mankind, and not embarrass'd with the Pride, Luxury, Ambition and Envy of the upper part of Mankind.

Defoe, however, could no more follow his own precepts than Crusoe could obey his father's counsels. He was an exceptional man, an artist in spite of himself, and in its own way the style he developed has very seldom been improved on. *Robinson Crusoe* and *Moll Flanders* each purport to tell a plain, unvarnished story, but into his narrative Defoe is perpetually slipping some revelatory detail or dramatic image. He might try to write like an honest, straightforward tradesman; he could not help seeing and feeling like an artist, and recording what he saw—he had an exquisite gift of observation—with an imaginative artist's skill and delicacy. When Crusoe is first cast up on his island, he thinks of his comrades who have perished in the storm: "as for them, I never saw them afterwards, or any Sign of them, except three of their Hats, one Cap, and two Shoes that were not Fellows."

It is the last detail that accents the whole passage; the fact that the shoes he picks up are "not fellows" strengthens his increasing sense of solitude. Similarly, the terrors that sometimes beset him are epitomized in the story of the "monstrous frightful old He-goat," whose "two broad shining Eyes" gleam out at him from the dusky hollow of a cave, and whose death rattle—"a very loud Sigh, like that of a Man in some Pain . . . follow'd by a broken Noise, as if of Words half express'd, and then a deep Sigh again"—brings Crusoe to a sudden standstill and makes him sweat with fear.

The description of the single footprint he finds in the sand is one of those passages in European literature that have left a permanent mark upon the human memory—symbolic scenes that seem to transcend fiction and to become a part of life itself. Once more Crusoe is terrified: "after innumerable fluttering Thoughts, like a man perfectly confus'd . . . I came Home to my Fortification . . . terrify'd to the last Degree, looking behind me at every two or three Steps . . ." Such an adventure never happened to Selkirk, and it is interesting to see how the novelist, while making the most of the material on which his story was based, has transfigured and enlarged his theme.

Crusoe, too, has been a sinner and a wanderer, enveloped in "a certain stupidity of Soul, without desire of good or conscience of Evil"; but unlike Selkirk, who, after he had been released from his island, soon drifted back into his old courses, he is a highly sensitive and well-organized man, possessing a remarkable capacity for self-discipline. To call Alexander Selkirk "the real Crusoe" is to misunderstand the nature of the artist's business. The true artist must always adapt; he reshapes a theme to suit his private purposes. Defoe, who shifted Selkirk's island from the South Pacific toward "the Mouth of the Great River of Orinoco" and condemned Crusoe to an imprisonment of "eight and twenty years," whereas his "real" counterpart had suffered only four years and four months, took everything that was memorable in the personality of Alexander Selkirk and, blending it with much that was memorable in himself, formed the full-length portrait of a modern hero.

ALI AND ALA

SWISS FAMILY ROBINSON

CONZETT & HUBER, ZURICH

The Robinsonades

The legend of Robinson Crusoe has had a tenacious hold on the imaginations of many men—and certainly of many children. The tale has been repeated, translated, and endlessly adapted. In the opinion of Jean-Jacques Rousseau, *Robinson Crusoe* was an ideal textbook for the young student of botany, zoology, agronomy, and morals. Throughout the eighteenth and nineteenth centuries there appeared a score of children's books on the Crusoe theme. *Ali and Ala*, a Swiss version by Johann Tobler, subtitled "An Attempt at a Truthful Cultural History for Young People," features a brother and sister whose parents take them away to an island in order to give them a natural upbringing. One of many French Robinsonades was *Robert on the Sea of Ice*, in which a young sailor is abandoned on an Arctic island. He eventually sends his diary off to sea in a bottle and is rescued by his own mother. A feminine Crusoe was invented in 1845 by a Frenchwoman, Madame Woillez. The heroine of her story, *Le Robinson des Demoiselles*, shipwrecked with her dog, discovers other castaways on her island, including a young orphan whom she rears. Almost as celebrated as Defoe's original is *The Swiss Family Robinson*, set on a tropical island, which Rudolph Wyss invented to amuse his children, one of whom arranged to publish the work in 1813. In the illustration below, Fritz, the eldest Robinson brother, is aided by his pet eagle in the slaying of a tiger.

ROBERT ON THE SEA OF ICE

LE ROBINSON DES DEMOISELLES

Visitors to a Pistoletto show get right into his paintings

Few serious painters would invite the public in to view an unfinished painting. The converse is true of Michelangelo Pistoletto, a thirty-three-year-old Italian artist: his paintings are not complete until the doors of the gallery are opened. The reason is as simple as his technique. Pistoletto paints on highly polished steel surfaces that reflect the audience in an infinite number of relationships with the figures in the paintings.

Pistoletto became involved in illusionary art about four years ago, while preparing a series of compositions on backgrounds of gold, silver, and bronze paint. One day he was "dumbfounded" by the movement of his own reflection across the painting. The discovery led to a process by which life-sized photographs were transferred to tissue silhouettes, worked up with soft pencil or paint, and then mounted on steel sheets. Our photographs show how visitors to his first one-man show in the U.S. got into the pictures.

The reflection of a young visitor at Pistoletto's show in Minneapolis (above) becomes for a moment a part of his painting of a picket line. At the right, she moves in to confront the flag-bearer.

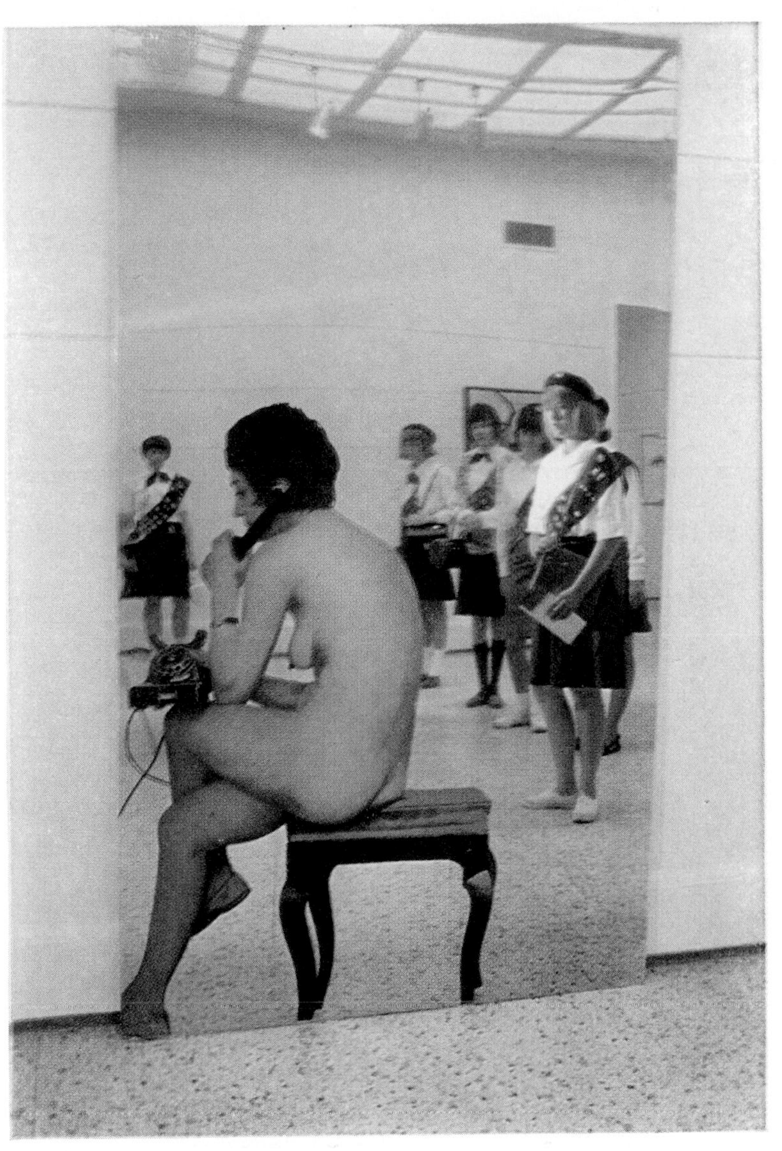

Members of the audience find it almost impossible to escape involvement in the art. At left, a group of Girl Scouts from Wisconsin eavesdrop on the Nude Woman Telephoning, *while a young man (at bottom) cautiously approaches the* Seated Woman. *Directly below, a* Man with Cigarette *is surrounded by a girl visitor and her own smiling reflection.*

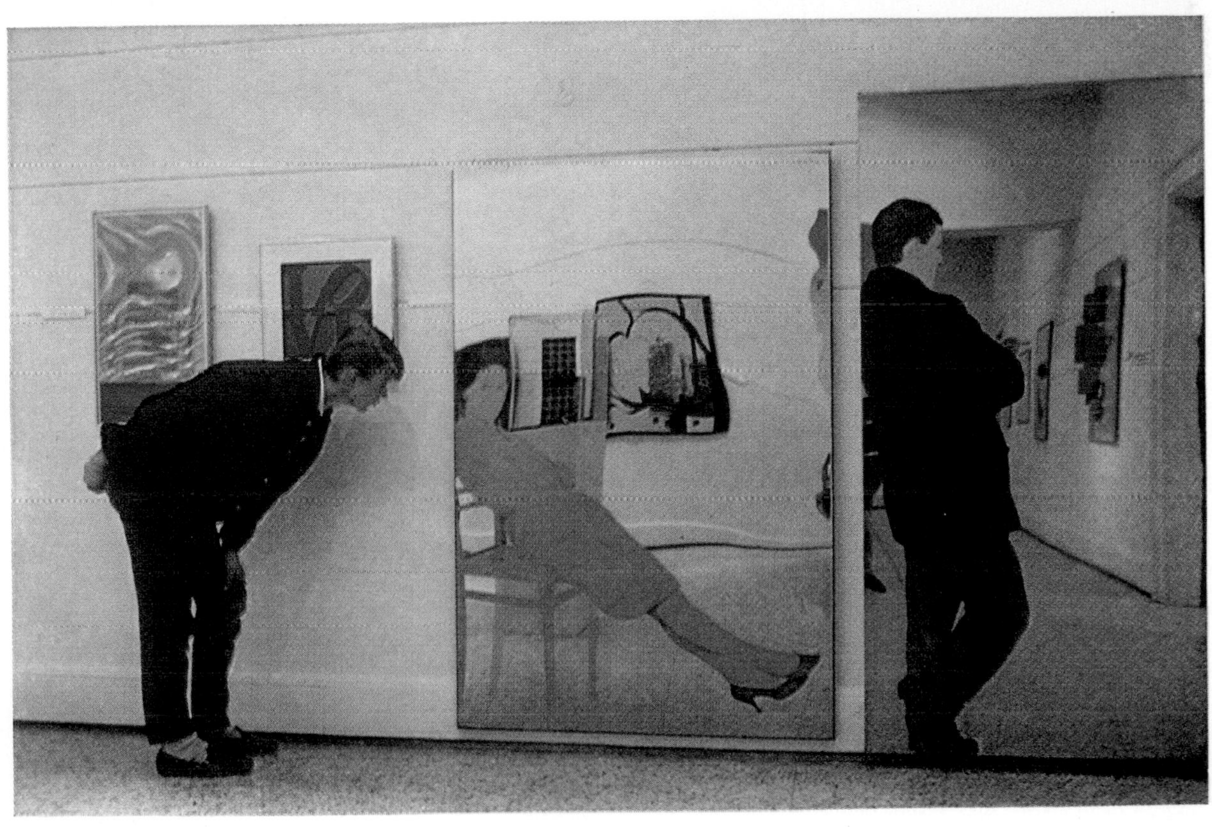

Photographed for Horizon at the Walker Art Center, Minneapolis, by Basil Langton

Andrew Wyeth turns his attention from landscapes to portraits

GRAPE WINE, 1966 (25½″ × 29¼″)

MAGA'S DAUGHTER, 1966 (26¾" × 30½")

The eighteenth-century Quaker hat had been lying around their house in Chadds Ford, Pennsylvania, for years. At one point Andrew Wyeth had considered painting it as a still life. But then one day his wife Betsy—who frequently appears in Wyeth's paintings—plopped the hat on her head; for the artist, present and past were vibrantly united in what he has called "time holding its breath." The result was *Maga's Daughter* (above), a tempera portrait in which Wyeth again demonstrates his extraordinary ability to find new meaning in the familiar.

Willard Snowden has also posed for Wyeth on more than one occasion. Chance brought the former sailor to Chadds Ford and a job taking care of Wyeth's studio; their association led to a memorable dry-brush character study, *The Drifter*, in 1964. Wyeth repeated his investigation of Willard the following year with *Monologue*, a title suggested by his helper's habit of talking through the sittings—"... about wine, mostly," Wyeth remembers. "He was worried about holidays. 'They should be kind to the human race,' he said to me. 'They should have the package stores open on Easter.' " Behind his dark beard and enigmatic expression, Willard Snowden is a timid and retiring person, whose character Wyeth masterfully probes in a new tempera, *Grape Wine* (opposite).

Until three years ago, Wyeth's name —the most famous in contemporary American painting—was not readily associated with portraits. In his concentration on the subject matter around Chadds Ford and his summer home in Cushing, Maine, the forty-nine-year-old artist has steadfastly refused portrait commissions. Does Wyeth's recent portraiture represent a new phase in his career? Yes, says Edgar P. Richardson, the director of the Winterthur Museum, who wrote the catalogue for the latest and largest Wyeth retrospective, assembled recently by the Pennsylvania Academy of Fine Arts in Philadelphia. Wyeth's "portraits of people in life size, rather than as elements in a landscape," Richardson maintains, have strengthened the artist's powers of observation and feeling. "All the qualities of his earlier work are there but are now intensified. ... Happily there is more to come."

THE ELEMENTAL TURNER

YACHT APPROACHING THE COAST, C. 1840–45 (40½" x 56")

Earth, air, fire, water—the English genius united them in paintings that hinted of the chaos of Creation

If England has produced a single genius among its many painters of talent, intelligence, and originality, that genius is Joseph Mallord William Turner. Alone among English painters Turner had "exceptional natural capacity for creative and original conceptions" (the dictionary's definition of genius) to a degree that is inexplicable and that can only be accepted as an independent phenomenon, self-generated and self-sustaining.

The extent of Turner's originality has been revealed only gradually by the series of aesthetic revolutions that have transformed our way of looking at art since his death in 1851. His long career carried him from realistic beginnings to an abstract conclusion, which is also the history of modern art. The impressionists were the first painters to discover that Turner had anticipated them; his water colors have been compared with Cézanne's. The cubists, it must be admitted, have been unable to tie their art to his, but the abstract expressionists and "action" painters of the 1950's and the new colorists of the 1960's have claimed him not only as an ancestor but even more enthusiastically as a colleague.

And yet, during the second half of the nineteenth century and the first part of this one, Turner's art had very little direct influence on the various painters or schools who seem to be descended from him. He has been discovered after the fact of revolutions rather than as a point of departure. The late sketches in which his originality seems most emphatically declared were not exhibited at all until 1906, and not in any quantity until 1938. After that, Turner's official canonization had to wait another twenty-eight years until, in 1966, the Museum of Modern Art in New York exhibited him, not as a nineteenth-century romantic, which he was, but as a twentieth-century abstractionist, which he can be made to seem by selecting certain bits and pieces of his work and thereby reducing the tremendous field of his art to the dimensions

Yacht Approaching the Coast *(left), one of Turner's late oil sketches, was painted for his own enjoyment and was not exhibited in his lifetime. It is an example of the style admired today for its similarity to contemporary abstraction.*

By JOHN CANADAY

of a mere studio exercise.

His field was the universe, and in discovering it he reversed the Biblical process of its creation. As a young artist he saw the world as the comfortably inhabited landscape of England, but as an old man he painted it as a spectacle of the four elements. Air, fire, and water fuse and spin around a vortex within which all solid forms have dissolved, but which could also serve as the primordial womb of force from which the earth was born. Whatever he understood of theory—or, more accurately, whatever he applied—was negligible in the achievement of his ultimate expression. For every passage in his work that seems to conform to a theory there are hundreds that contradict it; he was an empiricist who fulfilled his genius over a long route which he covered inch by experimental inch.

COURTESY OF THE TRUSTEES OF THE TATE GALLERY, LONDON

Self-portrait, c. 1798, shortly before Turner became a Royal Academy member.

Turner was a competent artist in his early teens, a successful one in his twenties, a great one during middle age, and then a very great one until a brief decline just before his death at the age of seventy-six. We have become so accustomed to thinking of him in terms of modernism that it is always surprising to remember that he grew up in the eighteenth century: he was born in 1775, in Maiden Lane, where his father was a barber and wigmaker. If he was not born holding a pencil, he must have soon learned. By the time he was twelve he was already sufficiently conscious of his identity as an artist to be signing and dating some not very impressive topographical drawings (probably copies, although they were done in the country, where his parents had sent him, at the age of ten, to live with an uncle).

This signing and dating at such an early age can be recognized, without too much romanticizing, as the germ of Turner's feeling in maturity that his work was a unit. If some of it had to be separated from the rest by sales to make money, which he loved, he refused to sell at any price the paintings he considered his best. When he died he left the contents of his studio—some three hundred and fifty paintings (more than half of them unfinished) and nineteen thousand drawings—to the nation. Anyone who has visited the Turner rooms in the London museums knows that Turner was right. Whatever the beauty and the power of his individual paintings may be, their effect, as a single revelation, is overwhelming. A similar display by most artists, even great ones, would be only encyclopedic and exhausting.

At fourteen Turner was admitted, on probation, as a student in the Royal Academy Schools, and returned to live with his parents in London. (At about the same time he received some instruction from one Thomas Malton, a topographical water-colorist who is chiefly remembered because he is supposed to have advised Turner's father to teach the unpromising boy some useful trade, such as that of tinker or cobbler.) At fifteen Turner had a water color in the Royal Academy exhibition, and for the next sixty years he was always represented there except when, occasionally, he chose not to exhibit. At seventeen he was supporting himself by coloring prints for engravers. At eighteen he set himself up in his own studio. At nineteen he was still working at copying other men's drawings, though in the same year one of his own drawings was published as an engraving, which meant that he had been accepted in a field that could be a source of major income for an artist—and was, for him, for the rest of his life.

By the time he was twenty, Turner was well established among printsellers, was making money, and was conspicuous enough to be mentioned for the first time (of many) in the gossipy diary of Joseph Farington (1747–1812), a landscape painter whose daily jottings are a standard chronicle of the London art scene of the period. When he was twenty-one, Turner exhibited his first oil at the Royal Academy, and in the last year of the century, when he was twenty-four, he was elected to the Academy as an Associate member—at the earliest age permitted.

By hindsight we can recognize that the Turner-to-be was nascent in the early oils exhibited at the Academy. On the surface these followed closely enough the subject matter that landscape painters found popular and salable—scenic spots of local interest, frequently with the ruins that were so romantically appealing to tourists. But a picture of Dunstanburgh Castle (see page 94) is subtitled "Sun-rise after a Squally Night," and that is the real subject. Likewise, a view of Millbank (also page 94) is only secondarily topographical: the scene is one huge receptacle for moonlight. *Morning Amongst the Coniston Fells* was accompanied in the Academy catalogue by lines from Milton's *Paradise Lost* beginning, "Ye mists and exhalations," and these rise in the distance, an effect of nature that one day would engulf entire canvases in chromatic fantasies and lead Constable to say, half ridiculing and half admiring, that Turner painted with tinted steam.

RICHARD EURICH, LONDON

Elderly Turner at the opening of the Academy: silhouette by John Ruskin.

The most revealing of the literary quotations that Turner chose for the catalogues at this time accompanied a painting of Buttermere Lake (page 94) in the exhibition of 1798:

Till in the western sky the downward sun
Looks out effulgent—the rapid radiance instantaneous strikes
Th' illumin'd mountain—in a yellow mist
Bestriding earth—the grand ethereal bow
Shoots up immense, and every hue unfolds.

"And every hue unfolds" is a prophecy of Turner's development, just as the "yellow mist" forecasts a passion for that color so great that in his old age Turner was caricatured as a short, squat figure, his oversized head bearing a great handsome beak of a nose, with a bucket of yellow paint and a mop, swabbing away at a large canvas. Turner had borrowed the lines accompanying *Buttermere Lake* from James Thomson's *The Seasons* (*Spring*) seventy years after they were written. But as a description of a Turner painting they might have been even more appropriate in another forty years, when Turner had discovered the miracle of Mediterranean light and the technical means of apotheosizing it in paint. Light, by then, had become for him the ultimate dynamic force, the abstraction of what Thomson had thought of as the heart of nature.

Turner had also discovered Sarah Danby, the widow of a composer and organist, and had begun an affair with her about 1798, the same year as the exhibition of *Buttermere Lake*. The affair lasted at least ten years and produced two daughters to add to the three Sarah had already borne her husband. Maddeningly little is known about Sarah Danby, but since one of her legitimate daughters married a composer and organist of respectable standing, and since one of Turner's daughters, Evelina, married a respectable consular official, Sarah must be imagined as a woman who maintained a respectable position of her own. That the youthful Turner was a combination lover and protégé to this cultivated woman is entirely without foundation, but it seems likely all the same.

The picture of this ill-educated young man poring over Milton and Thomson (and, as it turned out, making his own efforts at versification), possessed of a charming mistress, and having brought himself by the age of twenty-five to a position of prominence on his own terms against the grain of the snobbish, competitive art world, is an impressive and happy one. But it is given a different cast by a fact of Turner's life that must have been of central importance, both then and for the rest of his life. His election to the Royal Academy, a professional triumph, coincided with a personal tragedy, his mother's final reduction to hopeless insanity.

In 1800 she was admitted to Bethlehem Hospital, and when she was discharged as incurable the following year, she was put into a private asylum where she died three years later. Turner left virtually no autobiographical comments, and the inadequate records of his contemporaries sound as if they were unaware of his mother's madness. But certainly it was not something that Turner accepted easily. Rather, it might have explained why, in spite of his strong sexuality, he never married; why, in spite of his success, he felt a basic insecurity that led him to grasp sources of income that he did not need and to hoard money; why, in spite of a few close friendships, he remained such a loner in a society where he could have been a lion.

Soon after Turner's mother was committed to Bethlehem, his father closed the barbershop and moved in with his son as a general handy man. Turner was utterly without social ambitions; he and his father lived simply, almost roughly, without any interest in the appurtenant luxuries of the successful Londoner—the fine furniture, the silver, the servants, and the parties. But whatever else they had in common, they shared a love of money for its own sake, which is usual enough among poor people who have begun to earn large sums. The two Turners developed a reputation for being misers, and there were stories about the shabbiness and squalor in which they lived. But this tolerance of primitive domesticity can be explained as a natural indifference on Turner's part to vanities that would only complicate his life by taking more time (and, always, more money) than they were worth. Turner was simply too busy to bother.

When he was twenty-seven, Turner was elected to full membership in the Royal Academy. He could sell anything he wanted to, and seeing no point in working through intermediaries, in 1804 he opened his own gallery in Harley Street, where he kept twenty to thirty works on exhibition. He also moved into a better house, although not a better-kept one, in Upper Mall, Hammersmith. Then, in a few years—in 1810—he took a large house in Queen Anne Street, which he eventually remodeled to include his gallery-salesroom.

He was constantly busy and constantly successful, but he was also constantly looking for something that eluded him as an artist. He traveled incessantly looking for it, seeming not to know quite what it was, except that the peaceful English countryside did not offer it to him. He could and often did paint landscapes of great serenity, but the closed horizons and the intimate pastoral comforts that so delighted Constable were cramping to Turner. He traveled through England, Wales, and Scotland. In 1802, when the Treaty of Amiens was signed and the restrictions on visits to the Continent were lifted, he headed straight for the Alps, letting Paris and the Louvre wait for a visit on his way home.

All these experiences were reflected in his paintings. He had seen avalanches, and storms at sea, and he alternated paintings of the destructive forces of nature with others of idyllic visions in which rural England was adapted to the combination of romanticism and formality that had kept the Frenchman Claude Lorrain a deity of the Academy. Turner never hesitated to challenge comparison with the old masters, and he challenged Claude on his own ground, not only with Claudian adaptations of local subjects but with historical pictures on an operatic scale, like the famous *Dido Building Carthage* of 1815 (see page 95).

But the catalyst was somehow missing. By his early forties Turner had been a professional artist for a full quarter of a century, and his preoccupation with the quality of light had been continuous. The catalyst—or the fuse that lit the explosion—was his first trip to Italy, in 1819, when he was forty-four. He stayed five months.

RAIN, STEAM, AND SPEED — THE GREAT WESTERN RAILWAY, EXHIBITED 1844 (35¾" x 48")

Turner was far beyond the stage when the Vatican, with its Raphaels and Michelangelos, and the other shrines of Renaissance art would mean much to him. He made the Italian trip to see the sights, the ruins of antiquity, and perhaps from a general curiosity and the restlessness that made him a traveler all his life. What he discovered was that there existed in this southern country a kind of light that belonged to him and his painting. He had conceived of the elements in storm—water in flood, earth in avalanche, air in hurricane—and now he saw that there could be a storm of light. He saw that solid objects might be consumed in a sparkle of brilliant, shadowless radiance in a way altogether different from their soft dissolving in the cool "mists and exhalations" of the north. As if to make the revelation complete, Vesuvius erupted and Turner hurried down to Naples with

COURTESY OF THE TRUSTEES OF THE NATIONAL GALLERY, LONDON

Turner merged storm and steam in this picture of a train crossing the Taplow-Maidenhead viaduct. It was probably the first major painting inspired by the industrial revolution.

his water-color box to make firsthand acquaintance with primeval fire as a destructive natural force.

Turner's work from now on, truly revolutionary in its increasingly rough surfaces of pure color, its sacrifice of solid form to immaterial substances, its cataclysmic subjects, increasingly puzzled and offended most critics. But Turner was invulnerable. He had already made a fortune. If nobody had bought the new pictures, it would not have made much difference, but there were assiduous Turner collectors in spite of the critics. Nor was Turner too badly wounded in his self-esteem. When he was irritated, he could demolish a critic or a poor, foolish questioner among his clients with a murderously contemptuous phrase—but ordinarily he did not bother. In his pictures for the Academy, he had frequently made concessions to popular taste; now and then he still did. He was not above repeating an old success for a ready sale.

What kind of man was Turner by this time, fifty years old and at the height of his success? From a portion of the evidence it would be easy to picture him as a solitary misanthrope, and certainly it would be wrong to deduce any character in which there was not a strong element of pessimism. His use of human figures, so often the tiny victims of cosmic cataclysms, is frequently given as evidence that Turner was preoccupied with the theme of man's frailty, the indifference of the gods, or of nature, to our puny fate. But the comment is never much more than postscriptural, and the figures themselves, usually ill-drawn, are likewise postscripts to the rest of the painting and rather obtrusive in their small way. As often as not, the figures, with whatever philosophical comment they carry, seem to have been introduced as concessions to the nineteenth-century public's feeling of unease when faced by a picture without some kind of human or narrative interest to cling to.

Occasionally Turner adopted moralistic themes, but when he did so there was always a special reason. *Dido Building Carthage* and its companion, *The Decline of the Carthaginian Empire*, took their themes from Thomson's long poem *Liberty*, and warned by historical example that a nation must preserve the virtues that made it great, or must fall. But this high-minded theme was only a corollary to Turner's deliberate intention of painting two pictures that could stand comparison with the masters of the past—especially Claude Lorrain. In spite of their themes the pictures themselves are notable only (and splendidly) for their pictorial worth. Their philosophical content is dependent upon the accompanying literary exposition.

This was always true of Turner, no matter what sops he threw to the public (and perhaps to himself) by tying literary or topical references to exhibited pictures. He began composing verses of his own for this purpose, and in 1812 there appeared the first quotation from a poem with the cheerless title *Fallacies of Hope*—supposedly a work of epic length that Turner dabbled with over the years, but a work that was never seen. The quoted lines were probably written for each occasion, and were quite embarrassingly ill-written. Turner's thin acquaintance with humanistic learning has been regarded as a disadvantage accounting for the feeble classicism of his mythological subjects, but more perceptively it has been recognized as an advantage that gave his originality full play.

But none of this tells us much about Turner's personality. For a man so famous, he managed to keep his private life private to a degree that has left him indecipherable. He wrote almost no letters and never went out in society. Did he have friends among the sailors and fishermen and women of the ports where he went to sketch? He used to hire small fishing boats to take him out in rough weather and once had himself lashed to the mast for four hours to

TEXT CONTINUED ON PAGE 96

FISHERMEN AT SEA, 1796

F.W.A. FAIRFAX-CHOLMELEY, C.B.E.

MOONLIGHT, A STUDY AT MILLBANK, 1797

TATE GALLERY, LONDON

BUTTERMERE LAKE, 1798

TATE GALLERY, LONDON

DUNSTANBURGH CASTLE, 1798

NATIONAL GALLERY OF VICTORIA, MELBOURNE

Turner's first oil exhibited at the Royal Academy was probably the one at top left. In this and the other early paintings above, his fascination with light had already emerged. The scene below belonged to a series the artist did on English cathedrals.

DURHAM CATHEDRAL, C. 1835 (17⅞" x 11⅝")

NATIONAL GALLERY OF SCOTLAND, PIERRE BOULAT © TIME INC.

NATIONAL GALLERY, LONDON

DIDO BUILDING CARTHAGE, EXHIBITED 1815 (61¼" x 91¼")

Before he had actually encountered Mediterranean light, Turner depicted it in operatic historical paintings (above). But when he finally saw Italy in 1819, he began to fill sketchbooks with delicate and economical water colors such as the one below.

BY PERMISSION OF THE TRUSTEES OF THE BRITISH MUSEUM

SAN GIORGIO FROM THE DOGANA, VENICE: SUNRISE, 1819 (8¾" x 12")

TEXT CONTINUED FROM PAGE 93

observe the natural effects of a snowstorm, wondering all the while, he admitted later, whether he would survive the experience.

The friends he is known to have had, respected his privacy. By the time he was thirty-five—and perhaps much earlier—he was making annual visits to his friend Walter Fawkes of Farnley Hall, Yorkshire—visits that continued until Fawkes died in 1825. During this time Turner had formed a friendship with the Earl of Egremont and had made some trips to his seat at Petworth. When Turner was fifty-four, his father died—in September, 1829—and he began, at Petworth, the most intensely personal expression of his genius.

For eight years, until Lord Egremont's death, Turner was a regular visitor at Petworth, and the paintings and sketches he did there—most of which were not exhibited during his lifetime and were unknown even to the collectors most interested in his work—are at once the most evocative and the most maddeningly unspecific records of Turner's oddly complex and hidden spirit. There is in the first place the significant coincidence of the death of Turner's father and the beginning of the Petworth experience. The rough old man had been his steady companion for thirty years; whatever he had supplied in the way of an emotional center for his son's life must somehow have been transmuted to the unexpected quarter of Petworth, whose master was a connoisseur and collector.

The Petworth pictures represent Turner's first complete release into pure color as a field of light; in them he also becomes the technician who approximated pure abstraction in his treatment of paint simply as paint. But in every other way the Petworth pictures contrast with the rest of his work. Many are interiors, for one thing—great halls or intimate corners of bedrooms sometimes recognizable as rooms at Petworth but as often fantasies derived from them. The mood is warm and vibrant rather than violent, and—most exceptional of all—the scenes are dominated by the presence of human life. The human figures, it is true, dissolve into light along with architectural motifs and furniture, all consumed in yellows, oranges, and vermilions like live coals but without the violence of fire. Yet they are at home.

When Egremont died, Turner was sixty-two, and the year, 1837, marked the end of what must have been the happiest part of his life. The last oil painting he did there, *Interior at Petworth*, is of a vast imaginary hall, shattered and melting in golden light, and filled with the breath of spirits—an apotheosis and a farewell.

In 1828 Turner had made a second Italian visit; he made others, including at least two more to Venice. His big house and gallery on Queen Anne Street had acquired a housekeeper named Hannah Danby, a niece of Sarah's. (One is left wondering whether, or how, or when, Turner saw his daughters, or anyone else con-

TEXT CONTINUED ON PAGE 105

TURNER: A GRAVURE PORTFOLIO

"The artist delights to go back to the first chaos of the world," the critic William Hazlitt wrote of Turner's work in 1816, "or to that state of things when the waters were separated from the dry land, and light from darkness, but as yet no living thing nor tree bearing fruit was seen on the face of the earth." Hazlitt called him "the ablest landscape-painter now living," but shared the concern of many of his contemporaries over Turner's increasing tendency toward abstraction. "All is without form and void. Someone said of his landscapes that they were *pictures of nothing, and very like*." Though that process would only accelerate as the years went on, Turner the romantic and visionary would never totally divorce himself from form and subject: if he was ahead of his time, he was also very much a part of it. On the following eight pages Horizon reproduces a selection of Turner paintings spanning his career.

The elegiac *Peace—Burial at Sea* is a memorial to Turner's contemporary, the portrait and genre painter Sir David Wilkie, who died in 1841 and was buried at sea off Gibraltar. One recent critic has commented that the painting was "not only a tribute to fame and friendship; it was also a sly demonstration of how to use black." In his early painting *Calais Pier* Turner conveyed the excitement of a stormy day on the English Channel he knew so well; the mundane preparations of French fishermen and their wives are presented on an almost heroic scale. (Turner's contemporaries, however, criticized his rendering of the wave-chopped waters as mere "soap and chalk.") As time went on, the artist became more and more fascinated with the destructive forces of nature, in particular with the interaction of fire and water. The burning of the Houses of Parliament in October, 1834, was an event tailor-made to his preoccupation. Turner rushed to the scene, and dashing from one side of the Thames to the other, made quick water-color notes. He painted several versions of the holocaust, including the one reproduced here.

An idyllic contrast is his painting of the Venetian lagoon entitled *The Dogana, San Giorgio, the Zitelle*. From right to left, the Dogana, or customhouse, the Zitelle church, and Palladio's great domed San Giorgio Maggiore with its campanile are almost submerged in a shimmer of white light. But in *Shade and Darkness* water and light merge in a wild vortex. One of Turner's late and most abstract oils, it was based on Goethe's color theories, which had recently been translated into English. The painting is dominated by what Goethe called "minus colors" (blues, blue-greens, and purples), which, the German writer thought, produced "restless, susceptible, anxious impressions"—surely an apt description of the effect produced by a Turner painting.

PEACE—BURIAL AT SEA, EXHIBITED 1842 (34¼″ X 34⅛″)

CALAIS PIER, WITH FRENCH POISSARDS PREPARING FOR SEA: AN ENGLISH PACKET ARRIVING, EXHIBITED 1803 (67¾" X 94½")

BURNING OF THE HOUSES OF PARLIAMENT, EXHIBITED 1835 (36½" X 48½")

THE DOGANA, SAN GIORGIO, THE ZITELLE, FROM THE STEPS OF THE EUROPA, EXHIBITED 1842 (24¼″ X 36½″)

SHADE AND DARKNESS—THE EVENING OF THE DELUGE, EXHIBITED 1843 (30½″ X 30½″)

TEXT CONTINUED FROM PAGE 96

nected with his early affair with Sarah.) Hannah, a woman of notoriously repellent aspect, succeeded Turner's father as general factotum in the increasingly neglected house. It was frequently difficult for visitors to gain admission to the gallery, and Turner dispensed even with the small amenities he and his father had enjoyed. Two years after the death of Egremont, he took a cottage at the corner of Cremorne Road and Cheyne Walk in Chelsea, where he spent most of his time incognito. When he died there on December 19, 1851, the neighbors still knew him only as Admiral Booth, a retired officer who had taken to drink, and knew the woman he lived with as Mrs. Booth.

Turner seems, indeed, to have taken to drink, but only at the very end. The years after 1840 produced some of his consummate expressions, although toward the last he became, for the first time in his fifty years as a prominent artist, dull and heavy-handed. He exhibited four pictures at the Academy the year before he died, and even in the year of his death he managed to attend the varnishing days—the occasions when, often, he had completed his canvases as they were being hung on the wall.

Turner left an estate of £140,000, which would be more than three million dollars today. During his life he had never given much sign of interest in the artist's position in society, but he left funds to establish a foundation that would care for indigent artists. It died in the courts, but his daughters, after some legal complications, fared well. He was buried in St. Paul's.

One of the few critics who had any idea what Turner was about during his lifetime was John Ruskin, who was forty-four years younger and whose major book, *Modern Painters*, was initiated in 1843 as a defense of Turner. But modern critics have more than made up the difference by a tendency to exaggerate his modernism. Perhaps that is not quite the right way to put it: the modern critic tends, rather, to concentrate his attention on Turner's innovations while ignoring the expressive ends that these innovations served.

As a proto-impressionist Turner worked with gobbets of color, but he held to no theories of broken color and in his view of the world was about as far as possible from the impressionists. Turner's goal was always epic, never intimate. He was interested in Goethe's color theories, and worked out charts to analyze them, but in the end it was Goethe's ideas on the emotional associations of colors and not their physical characteristics that affected him. Turner's closest connection with what would be the impressionist technical revolution was his method of creating luminous effects by painting entirely in light tones rather than in contrasts of deep shadow and bright color. He thus identified light with pigment—the most generalized statement of the impressionists' technique—but whether he was or was not a major influence on

THE GUILD OF ST. GEORGE

Varnishing day at the Royal Academy was the occasion when an artist was allowed to put final touches on his paintings before exhibition. Turner, shown in this 1846 cartoon, sometimes used the opportunity to paint much of a picture.

Monet, who saw Turners in London in 1870, is a question that has two answers, depending, usually, on whether you are reading a French art historian or an English one.

Turner's approach was empirical no matter what his preliminary theories. The diarist Farington was saying something of the kind when he wrote that "Turner has no settled process but drives the color about till he has expressed the idea in his mind." Turner probably wouldn't have put it that way himself, but the business of "driving the color about" has been quoted to establish him as a distinguished grandparent of abstract expressionism, particularly the branch of it called "action" painting. There is a healthy germ of a relationship here: the late Turner paintings of storms, where the paint swirls in a great vortex, need only the slightest push to become totally abstract instead of abstractions based on nature, in which the elements are still discernible in their cosmic majesty. This recognition of subject, however, makes all the difference: at his most abstract, Turner is still employing abstracted pattern and abstracted color as a means to a specific and defined expressive end. He is not dealing with an aesthetic problem in which the means become the end in themselves—which is the exciting convenience, and the great tragedy, of contemporary art.

This tenth in a series by John Canaday, art critic of The New York Times, *is adapted from a section of his forthcoming book* Lives of the Painters *(W. W. Norton & Co.).*

MARIE ADELAIDE: VERSAILLES—SERVICE PHOTOGRAPHIQUE; LOUIS XIV: VERSAILLES—GIRAUDON; FRAME: N.Y. PUB. LIB. PRINTS DIV.

THE TWILIGHT PRINCESS AND THE SUN KING

There is a fairy-tale quality about the story of Marie Adélaïde of Savoy, the Italian Dauphine. But for the aging Louis XIV, not even her enchantments could hold off the darkness

By JOSEPH BARRY

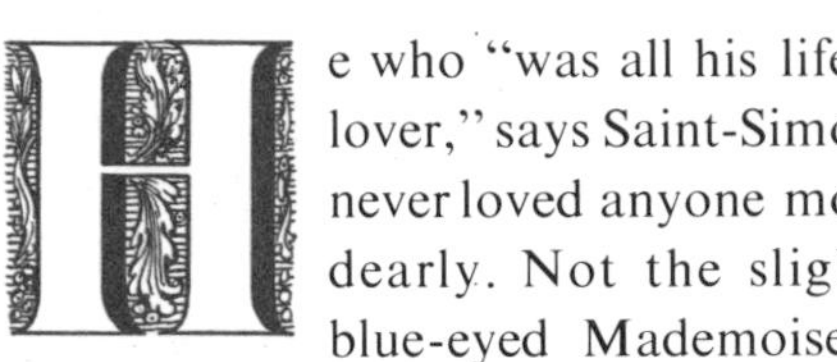

He who "was all his life a lover," says Saint-Simon, never loved anyone more dearly. Not the slight, blue-eyed Mademoiselle de La Vallière of his dawning grandeur, nor the dazzling Madame de Montespan of his high noon, nor, surely, Madame de Maintenon of his afternoon. Rather, the young Italian princess of his twilight.

Pietist Mme de Maintenon, whom the Sun King had probably married after the Queen's death, was twilight enough. But as the seventeenth century, which he had so long dominated, slowly turned, Louis XIV found Europe finally arrayed against him. Protestant England and Holland, Habsburg Austria and Spain, Sweden, Bavaria, the Palatinate and other German states, and Savoy.

Such was the dark political background of the darker personal story of Louis XIV and Marie Adélaïde of the Italian House of Savoy. She had come to France at the age of ten to marry Louis's grandson—the future Dauphin, the Duc de Bourgogne—and to bring a separate peace between France and Savoy. She was the granddaughter of Louis's brother, Monsieur, and his first wife, the unforgotten Henrietta of England, one of Louis's first loves.

When Marie Adélaïde arrived at Versailles, she brought a youth and gaiety to the aging court and King unknown since the days of her grandmother. When she quit it as Dauphine by way of death's door, the Duc de Saint-Simon sadly records, "darkness covered the face of the Court." Sorrow pierced the heart of the Sun King—"the only real sorrow that had ever entered into his life."

Perhaps it is the very sadness of the ending that gives the beginning of the story such legendary sweetness that autumn day of 1696 in Montargis. Marie Adélaïde had been driven to the border town of Pont-de-Beauvoisin, where she stayed in a house on the Savoy side of the river, and then had been taken across the bridge in her state coach. After she descended, a Savoyard page, bursting into tears, handed her train over to a French page.

While the princess and her new French household traveled toward Fontainebleau, the impatient Louis drove down as far as Montargis to meet her, arriving so early that he was at the door of her coach when it pulled up at six in the morning. He was charmed immediately. He would not, he told his brother, Monsieur, who accompanied him, change anything in her, and dispatched a courier in haste to tell Mme de Maintenon of his delight.

"I went to receive her in her coach," Louis wrote while the little princess rested. "She waited for me to speak, and then replied very well, but with a slight shyness which would have pleased you. I led her to her room through the crowd, allowing her to be seen from time to time by lighting up her face with the candelabra. This she supported with grace and modesty.

"Finally we reached her room, where there was a crowd and heat enough to kill one. I presented her from time to time to those who approached, and watched her from every point of view in order to tell you about her. She has the most graceful air and finest figure I have ever seen, perfectly dressed and her hair also, eyes bright and magnificent, eyelashes black and admirable, complexion smooth white and red, all that could be desired; the most beautiful black hair possible and in abundance. She is thin, as is proper at her age, mouth very red, lips thick, teeth white, long and irregular; hands well shaped but of the color of her age. She speaks little, at least as far as I have seen, and is not embarrassed when she is looked at, like one accustomed to the world. She curtsies badly, rather in the Italian fashion. . . . To speak to you as I am in the habit of doing, I find her perfect, and should be very sorry if she were more beautiful. I re-

In the cameos opposite, young Marie Adélaïde appears above Louis XIV

peat, I am pleased with everything except her curtsy. . . ."

Touchingly, the Grand Monarch adds: "Up to now I have behaved wonderfully. I hope I shall maintain a certain easy manner until we reach Fontainebleau."

At Nemours, the Duc de Bourgogne, barely fourteen, met his bride-to-be; both children were becomingly timid when the King presented them to each other. Scarcely taller, the solemn little Duc bent to kiss her hand—twice—and the little princess blushed. Then they all rode to Fontainebleau, arriving at four in the afternoon. The entire court was assembled on the great horseshoe staircase and a crowd stood below. "A magnificent sight," recalls Saint-Simon, to whom the petite princess, as the King escorted her, "seemed to be emerging from his pocket." Walking slowly along the terrace, introducing his charge to those who had the privilege, Louis led her to the late Queen Mother's apartment. Here in the princess's bedroom the Duchesse du Lude, henceforth her lady-in-waiting, had watchfully installed her own bed, as she was shortly to do at Versailles.

"Call me Monsieur, not Sire," Louis had told Marie Adélaïde, and ruled that she be called La Princesse, and that the Duc de Bourgogne be allowed to visit her only once every two weeks till the time of their marriage a full year later, and his two brothers only once a month. Soon, however, they were permitted a chaperoned half hour together every Saturday.

From Fontainebleau, Mme de Maintenon wrote the princess's mother: "She has a natural courtesy which permits her to say nothing but what is pleasant. Yesterday I tried to prevent her caressing me, saying I was too old. 'Ah, not so old as that!' she exclaimed, and did me the honor of embracing me."

Marie Adélaïde was even more familiar with the King. They played games together (he taught her how to play pall-mall). They drove together in the park. She sat on his knee, said "*tu*" to him, tugged at his chin, mussed his wig—and made few enemies at court. "Everybody," said Madame, Monsieur's second wife, "has become a child again."

Increasingly, remarks Saint-Simon, whose observations of his neighbors at Versailles had begun but a few years before, His Majesty delighted in the princess's spirit and precocity; he fixed the day of marriage for December 7, 1697, which fell immediately after her twelfth birthday. Though he had taken to dressing rather somberly those days, the King let it be known that he wished the court to be resplendent for the wedding, and ordered magnificent coats for himself. "As for Mme de Saint-Simon and myself," says the ducal memoirist wryly, "it cost us twenty thousand francs between us. There were not enough craftsmen to have everything finished in time."

Saint-Simon goes on to describe the conclusion of the wedding day: "The King and Queen of England [James II and his wife, living in exile as Louis's guests at Saint-Germain-en-Laye] came to dinner and the Queen sat between the two Kings. On leaving the table, the ladies went to see the bride's *coucher*, but the men were rigidly excluded by the King's command. . . . the Queen of England presented the nightgown, which was handed by the Duchesse du Lude. Mgr. le Duc de Bourgogne undressed in the ante-room, seated on a folding stool, attended by the King and all the princes. The King of England presented the shirt, which was handed by the Duc de Beauvilliers.

"When Mme la Duchesse de Bourgogne was in bed, Mgr. le Duc de Bourgogne [now fifteen] entered and got into bed on the right-hand side. . . . Immediately afterwards the King and Queen of England departed, the King retired to bed, and everyone left the chamber except Monseigneur [the young Duc's father who was then Dauphin], the princess's ladies, and the Duc de Beauvilliers, who stayed with his pupil, while the Duchesse du Lude stood at the other side. Monseigneur remained chatting for about a quarter of an hour, after which he made his son get up, telling him to kiss the princess, in spite of the Duchesse du Lude's objections. It turned out that she was right, for the King thought it very bad, saying that he did not wish his grandson to kiss so much as the tip of his wife's little finger until the time came for them to live together. He dressed again in the ante-room because of the cold, and went back to sleep in his own bedroom in the usual way. The little Duc de Berry [twelve], so naughty and bold, thought very ill of his brother's meekness in this respect. He said that he should have remained in bed."

Not long afterward, the Duc de Bourgogne did rebel at the arrangements. With the aid of a chambermaid, he hid in his little wife's closet and slipped into her bed when the Duchesse de Lude was asleep. But she awoke and ordered the prince to go back to his room. The following morning the Duchesse went straight to the King and complained. He summoned his grandson. "I have learned, Sir," he said, "that certain things have occurred which might be injurious to your health. I pray you see this does not happen again." "Sire," replied the Duc hastily, "I am very well." And the matter was not mentioned again.

After the marriage, the King gave a grand ball in the Gallery of Mirrors, with orange trees hung with hundreds of sugar-conserved oranges, and fireworks falling from the skies. Fete followed fete, with the Duc as Apollo and his young wife as a Muse, the Queen of Hearts, or a Chinese princess. Louis even gave her the menagerie at Versailles with its *fauves* and rare birds, cows, donkeys, and goats. Here Marie Adélaïde made cakes and played dairymaid à la Marie Antoinette a century later, churning butter for the royal breakfast—and everyone exclaimed on its flavor to please the King.

The Duc de Bourgogne seemed to shun such frivolities. Headstrong and vile-tempered as a child, under the guidance of his quietist tutor, the priestly Fénelon, he had become a studious, melancholy prince. It was Fénelon, too, who gave him the closest thing to a social conscience the age of Louis XIV could permit. "Each one," he told the boy, "owes infinitely more to the human race, which is the great country, than to the particular country in which he is born." Such teachings contributed to his being exiled to Cambrai as archbishop shortly after the princess appeared on the scene.

A contemporary print shows the marriage ceremony which joined (center) the twelve-year-old Princess of Savoy and the fifteen-year-old Duc de Bourgogne, the future Dauphin. The imposing figure (second from right) is Louis XIV.

BIBLIOTHEQUE NATIONALE—SERVICE PHOTOGRAPHIQUE

he Duc adored his wife (they were allowed to live together two years after the wedding), but abhorred the activities of the court. He disliked losing at cards; she lost often—the King looking on complacently. He disliked dancing; he had a slight limp from a twisted back which a corset of iron, called a "cross," hadn't helped. She enjoyed dancing enormously. "She would just as soon dance with an actor," Mme de Maintenon noticed, "as with a Prince of the Blood," and carefully limited the number of masked balls.

"M. le Duc de Bourgogne," observed Monsieur's shrewd second wife, Madame, "is so faithful that he cannot even look at another woman." And she recounts a tale as revealing of Versailles as of the young prince who was so out of tune with his times—and occasionally with his princess:

One evening Marie Adélaïde thought it would be amusing to play a joke on him, so she prevailed on Mme de la Vrillière to take her place in bed and then made a great show of being tired. The prince, overjoyed that for once his wife wanted to go to bed early, hurried to undress. He entered their bedroom and cried, "Where are you?"

"Here I am!" came the voice, muffled by the bedcovers.

Quickly the prince took off his dressing gown and slipped into bed. Then he saw the princess approach, fully dressed. "What, Sir, is this?" she exclaimed indignantly. "You play the saintly husband and here I find you in bed with one of the prettiest women of France!"

Slipperless and half naked, La Vrillière fled as the prince reached for one of his own slippers.

And Madame adds a note so typical of Versailles: "Those who came in to see what was going on tried to calm him down, but they were almost speechless with laughter."

Yet the portrait Saint-Simon has sketched of Marie Adélaïde remains that of a fairy-tale princess: ". . . she flitted hither and thither like a nymph, and like a summer breeze, she seemed to have the gift of being many places at once and brought life and gaiety wherever she passed." To anyone familiar with the difficult Duc de Saint-Simon, who even disdained the King on occasion, the praise, the unusual affection, is unexpected, but open-eyed:

"In appearance she was plain, [he writes of her later years] with cheeks that sagged, a forehead too prominent for beauty, an insignificant nose, and thick sensual lips, but the line of her chestnut hair and eyebrows was well marked, and she had the prettiest, most eloquent eyes in all the world. Her few remaining teeth were badly decayed, which she was the first to laugh at and remark on."

It makes a fascinating contrast to the King's portrait of the princess at ten. Saint-Simon continues, penetrating the "plainness" and explaining its appeal to contemporary taste:

"She had, however, a fair complexion, a beautiful skin, a small but admirable bust, and a long neck with the suspicion of a goiter, which was not unbecoming. The carriage of her head was noble; she was very stately and gracious in her manner and in the expression of her eyes, and she had the sweetest smile imaginable. . . . Her charm was beyond description. . . . When you were with her, you were tempted to believe that she was wholly and solely on your side."

Saint-Simon, one suspects, suspended his own ordinarily acid disbelief in telling us the princess was as pleased to spend a quiet afternoon reading and sewing, or conversing with her "serious ladies" (as she termed the older women of the palace), as playing cards or dancing. But at Versailles appearances were the important reality, and maintaining them the supreme achievement. Eventually that may have been what the fading Sun King valued most in his Italian princess.

In truth, the princess was more comforter to the old King, now in his sixties, than companion to her young husband. The King seemed to need her more; he would sit unusually solemn and silent, even at his public suppers, when her pleasure parties, which he himself encouraged, took her from his side. As a result, she was careful about mentioning them in his presence and made a point of seeing him before and after. If she returned too late, she would arrange to be with him when he awoke.

"The King desires Mme la Duchesse de Bourgogne to do exactly as she pleases from morn to night," the Marquis de Coulanges wrote to Mme de Sévigné's daughter, "and he feels rewarded if she is happy. So life is a constant succession of expeditions to Marly and Meudon, comings and goings to Paris for operas, balls and masquerades, and the gentlemen are practically at dagger's point trying to attract the princess's favor."

That was on February 2, 1700. The century of Louis XIV was still to take a long time dying.

n the ninth of November the French monarch received an urgent message from his ambassador in Madrid: the Spanish king, Charles II, had died without an heir. Though a Habsburg, three weeks previously he had signed a will leaving his throne to the second of his great-nephews, the Duc d'Anjou, Louis's grandson and the Duc de Bourgogne's brother. For a week Louis hesitated. If he accepted, it would probably mean the revival of the war with the first Grand Alliance, which had barely ended. If not, Habsburg Austria would inherit the Spanish throne, France would be surrounded, and there would probably be a war in any case.

Louis accepted. The eleven-year-long War of the Spanish Succession was the result. England, Holland, and Austria formed the second Grand Alliance against France, joined by most of the German states; Portugal and Savoy sided with France and Spain, then shifted to the allies in 1703.

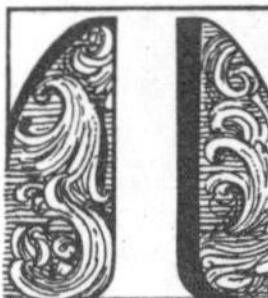hese were the darkest days of Louis's reign. But appearances had to be kept up. In war the serenity of the Sun King was worth battalions. Typically, after the shattering defeat at Blenheim, when thirty thousand of a French army of fifty thousand fell before Marlborough, Louis had Marie Adélaïde go to Paris to see a display of fireworks.

These were the years of forced growth—for the prince as for the princess. From Cambrai, Fénélon cautioned him not to sin by an excess of piety. "A great prince," he wrote, "has not to serve God as a hermit." And Louis sent his grandson off to serve France in Flanders. (There, one of the officers said to the Duc, "You will certainly win the Kingdom of Heaven, but as for winning the kingdom of this world, Marlborough and Prince Eugène [his ally] set about it in a better way.")

It was the princess who now turned to prayer, writing her husband constantly, "her heart beating at the arrival of every courier, fearing for his life, for his reputation" (as Mme de Maintenon said), and defending him at court. It was not easy for one whose father was at war with her husband and family, and she paid, in addition to everything else, a posthumous price—an accusation, never proved, that she sent military secrets to her father's House of Savoy.

There was another price the princess paid for her life and love with that complex man, the king of France. In 1704 the Duchesse de Bourgogne gave birth to a boy who died in less than a year. Two years later she gave birth to another who lived five years. And in 1710 she gave France its next king, Louis XV. In between, in 1708—but let Saint-Simon tell it:

"Mme la Duchesse de Bourgogne was pregnant; she felt extremely unwell. . . . [The King] wanted to make the usual Marly excursions. His granddaughter amused him, he would not go without her, but traveling was bad for her condition. Mme de Maintenon grew anxious. Fagon [the King's doctor] put in a discreet word. This merely irritated the King, who was not used to being crossed and had been spoiled by his mistresses, who had always accompanied him on journeys, even when pregnant or just risen from child-bed . . . The most he would concede was to defer twice the one arranged for Low Monday, and he insisted on going on the Wednesday of the following week despite all that could be said or done to stop him, or to gain permission for Mme la Duchesse de Bourgogne to remain at Versailles."

The result was a miscarriage. The news was broken to the King in the gardens in the presence of most of the court.

"M. de La Rochefoucauld protested out loud that it was a thousand pities, since she had miscarried before and might well have no other children. 'And if that should happen,' interrupted the King furiously, 'what do I care? She has one son already, has she not? And if he dies, is not the Duc de Berry of age to marry and have children? Why should I mind who succeeds me; are they not all grandchildren of mine?' Then with sudden rush of impatience, 'Thank God that she has miscarried, since it was bound to happen! Now, perhaps, I shall not be thwarted in my excursions and everything else that I want to do, by doctors' orders and midwives argufying. At last, I can come and go as I please and they will leave me in peace.' A silence during which you might have heard an elephant walking succeeded this outburst. . . . [It] lasted for fully a quarter of an hour. It was the King himself who broke it by leaning over the balustrade and speaking of a carp. No one answered him. Thereafter, he addressed his remarks about carp to the gardeners, who were not usually included in his conversation, and then he only spoke to them of the carp."

The next year there were fresh misfortunes. It froze. It froze for seventeen days. The Seine and the sea around the coast froze. Olive and orange trees froze. Grain, cows, goats, sheep, chickens, even rabbits, froze. It was a year of famine. It was a year of defeats: eleven thousand Frenchmen died at Malplaquet. The nobles turned in their silver plate. Stranger still, the people responded to Louis's appeal with recruits and valuables, and France somehow carried on. The princess was constantly with the King; he found her "capable of difficult and important things."

n the eighth of April, 1711, Monseigneur (the Dauphin) saw a priest carrying Communion to a dying man. He descended from his coach with the Duchesse de Bourgogne and knelt before the priest. A week later he was dead from smallpox. Louis went to Marly and wept in the dark. The next morning he named his grandson, not yet thirty, Dauphin. The Duchesse became the Dauphine. They now stood on the steps of the French throne.

The new Dauphin was suddenly a changed man. Gone, as if overnight, were the shyness and timidity. He took his place at court, attended all Council meetings, worked hard, won the respect of the King, and prepared for what seemed his destiny. When Louis offered him his father's monthly allowance of 50,000 francs, he said he was content with his 12,000. He asked to be called Monsieur, not Monseigneur, and persuaded Louis to order an inquiry into the state of the nation. It filled forty-two folio volumes. "There can be no rest for a King," he noted, as he studied them. But he had never been happier.

On the eighteenth of January, 1712, still in mourning, the seventy-three-year-old King took his court to Marly. The Dauphine had arrived earlier, her face "hugely swollen," and immediately went to bed. At the King's request, however, she rose at seven to preside over the drawing room, her head swathed in a hood as she played cards. Then she returned to bed, where she ate supper.

The following day the Dauphin received a letter from his brother, the king of Spain, warning him of poison. It greatly disturbed the twenty-six-year-old Dauphine. An Italian astrologer had foretold her death before twenty-seven, and she frequently recalled his words. "The time is approaching," she once told the prince. "Whom will you marry when I die?"

"No one," he said. "In a week I would follow you to the grave."

The next few days she felt better and on the first of February the court returned to Versailles. On Friday the fifth, the Duc de Noailles gave her a beautiful snuffbox with fine Spanish snuff. She tried it, liked it, and put it aside. That evening she had a fever and felt pain, and implored the King not to enter her room. She was given opium and bled twice from the arm. She sent one of her ladies-in-waiting for the snuffbox. It had disappeared.

On the eighth the red spots that were the sign of measles marked her body; the King came often to her bedside. On the tenth the Dauphin, who had never left her, was persuaded to go into the garden for fresh air; he came back almost immediately. Toward nightfall she became worse and spent a very bad night. The next day she was given the Last Sacraments. "Today a princess," she said resignedly, "tomorrow nothing." Seven doctors ordered her bled from the foot.

On the twelfth she was conscious only at intervals. Toward evening her servants became so distraught that many strangers were allowed into her room, even though the King was present. At eight o'clock she died. The King, as custom demanded, left the death chamber a few moments before, and drove to Marly with Mme de Maintenon to be alone with his grief. He could not summon the strength to see or talk to the Dauphin.

Toward the end, he had been ordered by the King to keep away from his wife's bedroom, so that he might not catch the fatal fever. But on the fourteenth he looked so ill that Louis had the doctors take his pulse, and on the sixteenth the ominous spots appeared. "His sorrow at losing her broke his heart," says Saint-Simon, who had been horribly shocked by his stricken look the day after her death. "Onlookers saw a man, driven frantic with grief, who still wrung out of himself the strength to preserve a calm exterior but died in the struggle. His days were soon brought to a premature close."

t eight thirty in the evening, on the sixth day after his wife's death, he died. "In his death," mourned Saint-Simon, "France suffered her final chastisement, for God showed her the prince whom she did not deserve."

And of the princess he wrote: "With her death, all joy vanished, all pleasures, entertainments, and delights were overcast and darkness covered the face of the Court. She was its light and life. She was everywhere at once, she was its center; her presence permeated its inner life, and if, after her death, the Court continued to subsist, it merely lingered on. No princess was ever so sincerely mourned, none was ever more worth regretting. Indeed, mourning for her has never ceased, a secret, involuntary sadness has remained, a terrible emptiness that never can be filled."

Nor was it ever filled for the King. With her death, twilight became night, the war ended in compromise and exhaustion, and he prepared for his own death in the year that followed.

Joseph Barry went to France with Patton's Third Army, and, with one brief interlude, he has lived and written there ever since. Mr. Barry's latest book is The People of Paris, *which was published last fall by Doubleday & Company, Inc.*

Where is the Bridegroom?

Gilbert Highet presents his solution to a famous puzzle in Bruegel's *Peasant Wedding*

The painting shows a party of country folk celebrating a wedding by having a midday meal. Most of it is clear enough, amusing and sympathetic, easy to understand. For instance, right in the foreground, closest to the onlooker, a small girl about three years old sits on the floor eating from a plate with her finger and sucking the finger clean. She is dressed in ugly dark thick Flemish clothes, with plenty of petticoats and sturdy little boots, but she has a gallant peacock feather stuck in her hat because she has been taken to a party. These are simple, decent people.

The emotional tone of the painting is predominantly peaceful and harmonious. It is occasionally discussed together with Bruegel's *Peasant Dance* as though the two paintings expressed a similar spirit. That is a mistake. They make a sharp contrast. The dancers are excited, ungainly, rather drunk, their jollification coarse and boorish; even the composition of the group is involved and turbulent. But the *Wedding* is sedate. It is built on a long, smooth diagonal extending right across the picture—the table, prolonged by the tray in the immediate foreground. On each side of the table sit the guests, eating and drinking purposefully but in the main quietly. Their arrangement is orderly. At the extreme right are a man of distinction and a friar; at the extreme left, the humblest villagers, not even at table but gathered outside. No one is drunk. No one is dancing or even smiling. Most of the guests look stodgy but not unpleasant, and of the three faces in the foreground, two are decent, calm, and honest. This point must be made because critics commenting on the picture sometimes take it as a denunciation of coarse vices.

Thus C. G. Stridbeck (*Bruegelstudien*, Stockholm, 1956) sees the bagpipes as a symbol of Sin, the wooden spoons as symbols of Gluttony, and the little girl as a greedy guzzler. Without observing the complete difference of ethos, he compares this calm, respectable scene with a contemporary picture of a Beggars' Banquet in which the ragged guests are voraciously dissecting a roast pig, and a man in the immediate foreground, turning away from the table to face the spectator, is vomiting on the ground. No. There are a few jarring notes

By GILBERT HIGHET

In the winter issue, HORIZON *reproduced in color a detail from Pieter Bruegel's* Peasant Wedding. *For four centuries this famous painting of a rustic marriage feast has presented Bruegel's admirers with a puzzle: where is the bridegroom? In 1945, Gilbert Highet, who is now chairman of* HORIZON*'s Editorial Advisory Board, first presented his solution of the mystery in the late* American Magazine of Art. *From Bruegel scholars since that time, his view has brought both agreement and dissent. The continuing argument lends interest to Dr. Highet's solution, presented anew here.*

KUNSTHISTORICHES MUSEUM, VIENNA

in the *Peasant Wedding*, but in the main the people are quiet and decorous. They may be dull, but they are not besotted and vicious. Bruegel portrayed gluttony in a wonderfully comic engraving of a *Fat Kitchen* (1563) full of hams and sausages and plump cheeks and bulging bellies; nothing could be less like the *Peasant Wedding.*

The chief problem in the picture is this: although the bride is prominent, as she should be at her wedding, it is not easy to find the bridegroom. Bruegel placed the bride in the middle distance, but signalized her with perfect clarity. He set her head—the only bare head at the table—against a large cloth hung on the wall, emphasized it by hanging a bridal crown above it, and carried the spectator's eye toward her by the active gesture of the young man distributing food in the foreground. But the bridegroom does not appear to be accentuated in this way, and the experts differ about his identity, even about his presence. Gustav Glück, the editor of the fine Vienna album of Bruegel's paintings (1937), confesses he is at a loss. Baron Joseph van der Elst, in *The Last Flowering of the Middle Ages* (Garden City, N. Y., 1944), comments: "There is an old Flemish proverb: 'It is a poor man who is not able to be at his own wedding.' That seems to be the case here." Bruegel loved proverbs, but he would scarcely paint such a large and complex picture in order to illustrate such a weak little adage—which after all is simply a hyperbole like "It's a poor heart that never rejoices." Besides, it is not a poor man's wedding. The family may not be rich, but they have lots of food and drink and hospitality and can afford to pay two pipers. K. C. Lindsay and B. Huppé, writing in the *Journal of Aesthetics and Art Criticism* for March, 1956, suggest that the bridegroom is absent because the painting symbolizes ecclesiastical corruption. "The fleshy Bride, given to the world, conspicuously lacks her Bridegroom"; i.e., the peasant girl represents the Church and the absent groom corresponds to Jesus Christ. This is ingenious but scarcely convincing—chiefly because the tranquil mood of the picture does not suggest, at its first or at its hundred-and-first viewing, that the painter intended it as a denunciation of a mighty spiritual discord, comparable to *Piers Plowman.*

The bridegroom must be in the picture. If we can find him, we shall understand more of its significance. It is worth remembering that Bruegel was never afraid of telling stories in his paintings. He told them with as many rich details as a modern novelist. Some of his pictures take as long to read, and are as full of social commentary, as a book by Balzac. (Others are as wild, as complicated with incongruous imagery, as *Finnegans Wake;* but the *Peasant Wedding* is not among them.) He meant his spectators to study the spiritual meaning both of the details and of the ensemble in each picture. He would scarcely have understood why anyone except a student should devote an entire painting to a few apples in a bowl, however distorted and discolored. Yet the meaning of his pictures is never a platitude: there is nothing like "The Gambler's Wife" or "The Doctor." His *Peasant Wedding* is not a nice simple E flat major ceremony, like Karl Goldmark's symphony of the same name. Bruegel loved exploring contrasts and developing discords.

His wedding party is held at a farm, evidently the bride's home. Since the farmhouse is too small to accommodate all the guests, the meal is served in the barn. Everything is makeshift. We even have a slight feeling of embarrassment for the bride, who is so carefully dressed and yet has to celebrate her wedding in the barn, where she has often milked cows or stacked turnips. The room is only half of the barn. The other half is still full of hay, which forms the rear limit of the picture. Two sheaves and a rake are hanging in a fine decorative pattern on the wall of hay at the right. Perhaps these were the last sheaves of the harvest; as such they will be emblems of fertility, to be kept until the next harvest comes in. (The last sheaf was sometimes called the Maiden, or the Bride, says Frazer in *The Golden Bough.*) The bride's family has made an effort to set her off by hanging a curtain behind her, like the tapestry behind the seats of the lord and lady in noble families. It is not nailed up; it is slung from a rope stretched between a post and a pitchfork stuck in the hay. At the far left we can see more farm implements hanging up.

The seats, too, are improvised: benches, a stool, even an upturned tub; and the food is carried in, not on trays, but on a door taken off its hinges and supported on two poles. The floor has been swept clean; but, to remind us where we are, Bruegel has painted in the immediate foreground at the right, with exquisite detail, a single straggling straw.

The guests have reached dessert. Remains of the first course (bread and meat) are visible here and there on the table. Now the guests are getting *vladen*—custard pies—some plain and some flavored and colored with saffron. The drink is beer, served in large tankards. (A few critics call it wine, but Flemish farmers could scarcely afford wine in such quantities, even at a wedding, and if they could, would not serve it in tankards that hold at least a quart.)

Almost all the guests, dressed like the beplumed child in thick peasant clothes, are country folk. Only a few have distinctive costume. Bruegel intended these few to attract and retain our interest.

The bride herself is a healthy, blowzy

heifer, with an expression of self-satisfaction which is scarcely attractive. Most girls on their wedding day are either desirable or pathetic. She is neither. She is almost a parody of the Lovely Bride. She is not eating: she does not want to commit a *faux pas* by ingesting a large mouthful, or drinking beer and belching; and she wants her breath to remain sweet for tonight. With her downcast eyes, her clasped hands, her smooth hair, her red cheeks, her polite smirk, and the cockeyed crown hanging above her, she could be a travesty of the Madonnas of Flemish art. Bruegel was too good a painter not to have intended the resemblance.

The bride is in the middle distance, although carefully focused by Bruegel's composition. In the foreground there are only six figures. One is the child with the peacock-feather hat. Two are aproned servants carrying custard pies—they have their backs partly turned to us, so that Bruegel means us to think them less notable than the food they are carrying. The other three are all clear and prominent: two in full face, one in profile. All are evidently important.

Two of them physically resemble each other. At the head of the table is a quiet, serious young man with a red cap, who is busy taking dishes off the door-tray and handing them down the table. As though it were his special function to distribute food to the guests, the servants have stopped beside him. On the left is another young man with the same serious naïve face, engaged in a similar task, pouring beer out of a jeroboam into a tankard. The two young men look alike, and both look like the bride. All three have the same broad, flat face, a rather childish chin with a horizontal valley below the lip, a strong wide-nostriled nose, and, to emphasize the resemblance, the same downcast eyes. All have the same reddish fair hair. One of the young men is passing out food, and the other drink. One sits at the head of the table, with room beside him for the other—who has apparently risen to pour out the beer. There is a mysterious foot visible under the door-tray, belonging to nobody. A leading authority, Ludwig von Baldass, thinks Bruegel inserted it for the purpose of "opposing a counter-movement to the principal movement" (*Les Arts Plastiques,* 1948); but perhaps Bruegel originally put both brothers at the head of the table, and then, moving one to the bar-service, forgot to paint out his foot. Since they distribute food and drink, have prominent places at the table, and resemble the bride, these are the hosts—the brothers of the bride.

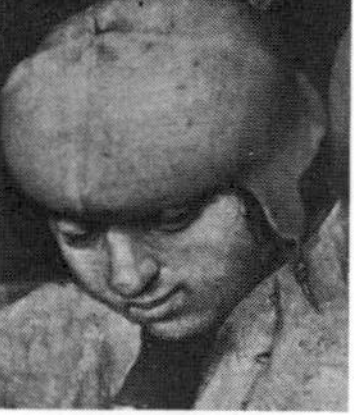

Before we look at the central male figure—a thin, peevish man holding a tankard—let us see who are the other guests of honor.

Far on the right, removed from all the country people, is a richly dressed man in his middle years. He alone has a beard. He alone wears a sword (or at least a hanger) with an ornamental hilt. He alone has a lace ruff, and trimmings (of white vair?) on his black velvet coat, and a pet hound. While the friar sitting beside him talks to him with an earnestness that betokens some respect, he listens with patient dignity. Rather pointedly, he keeps his hands clasped on the table top. He has come to the wedding as a compliment to the bride's or the bridegroom's family; but he will not eat or drink or converse with the other guests, and he sits morose and self-contained while the friar talks to him with the admonitory gesture of a preacher. He has put some morsels of food on the bench beside him, to occupy his dog, which noses at them without much interest. He is the local squire. The cata-

logue of the Archduke Leopold Wilhelm's collections (1659) mentions this picture and identifies him as a judge; some critics see in him the mayor of the village. Whatever the case may be, he represents a superior social class.

On the right of the friar are an elderly man and woman who look curiously like each other: well-dressed, thin, sharp, vivacious, intelligent, rather unattractive. The man, white-haired, has been given a special high-backed chair, and the woman is seated next to the bride. They are as important as the friar and the squire, but by their position they must have a closer connection with the wedding. They do not seem to be like the bride or her brothers. The man is not dressed like a farmer; he is not the host but a guest. Therefore they are the bridegroom's father and mother.

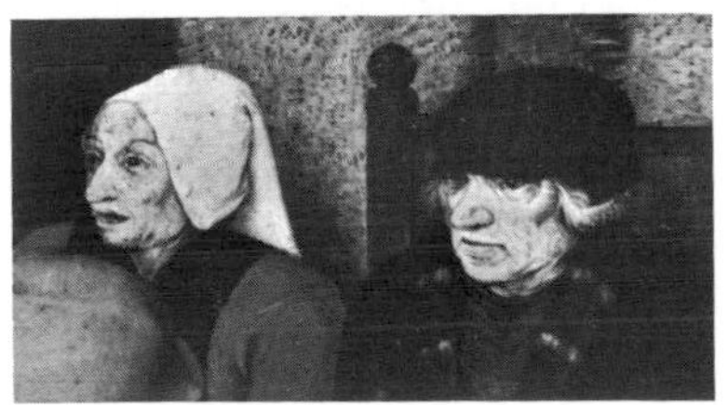

But where are the parents of the bride? Since her two brothers are playing the hosts, her father must be dead. The woman sitting at the right hand of the bride, in a position equal or superior to that of the groom's mother, has a distinctive coif. As she talks to one of the guests, her face is hidden by the head of a servant. She should be the mother of the bride.

Now, the bridegroom. Where is he? In desperation Gustav Glück says, "Perhaps he is the greedy gobbler half-way down the table with the spoon in his mouth." For this suggestion he offers no supporting reason; the implication is that since the greedy man is looking straight at the camera he must be important. Certainly we are meant to notice him. He is a comical fellow, and his startled gaze has a meaning. But he is not the bridegroom: he is mixed up with the ordinary guests and shows no sign of distinction except that flash-bulb stare—which is paralleled in the startled look of the foremost bagpiper.

There is only one person left. Right at the center of the picture, sitting beside the bride's brother and opposite the friar, is an ugly, well-dressed man with a disagreeable expression—such an unpleasant fellow that we instinctively dismiss him from consideration as the groom of the plump girl facing him. Nevertheless, he is made prominent by his position, by his costume, by his gesture and expression, and by the gaze of other members of the wedding. This is the bridegroom.

He has money. Only two other men wear those dark clothes. Everyone else is in rustic drab. The squire and the father-in-law and this man wear the dark formal garb of the gentleman, and of the bourgeois who never has to do manual labor or work in muddy fields. Even his hat (like the hat of the squire and of his father opposite) is more elaborate than those of the others. But his costume makes a marked contrast with his face and bearing. He is an ugly man with a hard, coarse mouth, lips partly opened in a peevish utterance—an expression emphatically similar to that of his father and mother opposite. He seems to have a big birthmark on his right cheek near the angle of the jaw.

Everyone else in the room is placidly eating or drinking, or serving, or tactfully abstaining. Only one person is calling for more and exhibiting dissatisfaction. The bridegroom is leaning back at an angle that differentiates him from the other guests, holding up his tankard, looking angrily at the servants, and bringing the bride's brother into the sphere of his indignation. "Why don't you bring me my beer? Don't you know who I am? Can't you hear me, you there?" His rude outburst has startled the popeyed man, who pauses with the spoon in his mouth, and one of the pipers, who stops to stare while his partner keeps on playing. It also annoys his mother and father. They glare at him across the table, the father silently, with glittering eyes and the beginning of a warning gesture, the mother with her lips parted to scold. The bride, with eyes downcast, and her brothers, busy hosts, have not heard, or prefer not to hear. But in this ill-tempered moment the bridegroom and his parents have the same nasty expression—vanity without dignity, wealth without grace. The parents are annoyed, but not surprised. They know their boy: he is something like Wenzel in *The Bartered Bride,* a spoiled son unfit to be a husband.

This is the point of the picture. It portrays the social disharmony of town and country. The girl has married above her. She will have a difficult life with that saw-edged mother-in-law, that rich and snarly father-in-law, that desiccated and selfish husband. How will she live when she moves into Antwerp and keeps house for that avaricious merchant? Will she be driven to distraction by his bad temper and his nagging parents? Or will she be contented because she need not stack turnips and pitch hay any more, because her children will have good black clothes and sit in carved wooden chairs instead of wearing peasant stuff and sitting on the floor? Her downcast eyes, her clasped hands, her smug smile, suggest the answer.

Willa Cather, "The Meatax Girl"

At twenty she sharpened her literary style on the hapless actors who found their way to the Lansing Theatre, Lincoln, Nebraska

BENNETT MARTIN PUB. LIB., LINCOLN, NEB.

Some young writers have developed their literary muscles on adolescent poetry, some on diaries, some, more recently, by writing television commercials. Willa Cather developed hers by pummeling actors and other writers, when in 1893, at the age of twenty, she began to produce theatrical and literary criticism for the *Nebraska State Journal,* published in Lincoln. She had not yet started writing her own novels, and she poured most of her energies, insights, and devastating wit into criticism. The result is a collection of essays selected and edited with a commentary by Bernice Slote (to be published in March by the University of Nebraska Press under the title *The Kingdom of Art: Willa Cather's First Principles and Critical Statements, 1893–1896*) that reads as well as many a novel and a good deal better than most criticism. Precocious young lady that she was, she was willing to take on anyone, and often tackled the acting companies that played at the Lansing Theatre in Lincoln—across the street from the "Shakespeare" pub. In 1921 Will Owen Jones wrote in the *Journal:* ". . . Many an actor wondered on coming to Lincoln what would appear the next morning from the pen of that meatax young girl . . ." Judging by the excerpts printed here, writers and actors at the turn of the century must have welcomed the change when Willa Cather gave up criticism in favor of novels. Others might wish she had kept on, and on, and on.

". . . a barge drew up and from it descended a large, limp, lachrymose 'Kleo-paw-tra,' with an Iowa accent, a St. Louis air, and the robust physique of a West England farmer's wife."

The serpent of old Nile uncoiled . . . last night before a large and amused audience. While the text was considerably mutilated in places, still the general outline of the play was recognizably Shakespearean. The fortune telling scene was put first and after that a barge drew up and from it descended a large, limp, lachrymose "Kleo-paw-tra," with an Iowa accent, a St. Louis air, and the robust physique of a West England farmer's wife. This ponderous personage descended from the barge and perching upon the back of a stuffed tiger somewhat moth-eaten she began gleefully coquetting with Mark Antony, recently of Rome, whom she occasionally called "Me Anthony," which showed that she had been reading *The Prisoner of Zenda.*

Mark Antony, impersonated by Edward Collier, was the only piece of legitimate acting in the whole production. In spite of a decided tendency to continually declaim and fling the Shakespearean lines about like banners, he has the conventional intelligent conception of his part and that is something, nay, in this company it was much.

The Enobarbus of George Wessell was certainly as remote as possible from that of Shakespeare. The real Enobarbus was a gentleman somewhat more shrewd than frank, wise in wine and women and wiser still in war, low of voice and smooth of tongue. Mr. Wessell shouted like a free silver advocate and that beautiful description of Cleopatra on the Cyndus [Cydnus], that paragraph that is almost as full of delicate poetry as Mercutio's Queen Mab speech, he mouthed as though he was shouting "Spartacus the Gladiator."

The gorgeous stage settings were certainly all that could be asked of a one-dollar attraction, but the crops must have failed in Egypt that year. During the battle of Actium the audience was treated to stereopticon views. It only needed a lecture. It's not every production of Cleopatra that's embellished by magic lantern slides. The bare-footed ballet was there, with both feet, but even it did not bring relief to the weary souls who longed for it.

And how was it with the rural, robust queen, the royal Kleopawtra? Miss Lewis walks like a milkmaid and moves like a housemaid, not a movement or gesture was dignified, much less regal. She draped and heaped her ample form about over chairs and couches to imitate oriental luxury. She slapped her messenger upon the back, she tickled Mark Antony under the chin. She fainted slouchily upon every possible pretext and upon every part of the stage. And it was no ordinary faint either, it was a regular landslide. When the messenger brings the tidings of Antony's marriage she treats him exactly as an irate housewife might treat a servant who had broken her best pickle dish. When she lavishes her affection upon Antony, she is only large and soft and spoony. To call her amorous would be madness, she was spoony, and it was large, two hundred pounds, matronly spooniness.

Her death scene was done in the modern emotional drama ten, twenty, and thirty-cent carnival style. She took a few tears from *Camille*, a few from *Article 47*, a few from *Credit Lorraine*, a few from *As in a Looking Glass* and made a death scene. She sat down upon a cane bottom dining room chair, took her crown from a little sixteenth-century oak table, sighed and wept and heaved her breast and then died from an imaginary serpent hidden in a ditch of lettuce after having worn most atrocious gowns and having drawn and quartered and mangled some of the greatest lines in all the poetry of the world. *Requiescat in pace*. Was ever Shakespeare in this fashion played?

". . . the only Cleopatra on earth worth the seeing . . ."

There was just [one] good thing about Miss Lewis' Cleopatra, and that was that, as hunger makes one dream of banquets, it recalled the only Cleopatra on earth worth the seeing, the royal Egyptian of Sarah Bernhardt. I could see it all again, that royal creature with the face of flame, every inch a queen and always a woman. The bewildering reality of that first scene with Mark Antony in which her caresses are few, fitful, unexpected, light as air and hot as fire. The regal queenliness with which she sends him from her back to Rome, when she touches his sword with her lips and invokes the god of victory, and one feels that in her veins there flows the blood of a hundred centuries of kings. And the restlessness of her when he is gone. . . . The madness of her fury when the messenger delivers his news, how her face became famished and hungry and her eyes burned like a tiger's and her very flesh seemed to cleave to her bones. How—but bah! it is not possible to describe it. It was like the lightning which flashes and terrifies and is gone. Through it all she keeps doing little things that you do not expect to see on the stage . . . She gives you those moments of absolute reality of experience, of positive knowledge that are the test of all great art. The thing itself is in her, the absolute quality that all books write of, all songs sing of, all men dream of, that only one in hundreds ever knows or realizes.

"It is not likely that he [Shakespeare] set up a great ideal and struggled to attain it. He wrote easily and carelessly, perhaps between drinks . . ."

It will be here again in a few days, that old 23d of April, on which it is written down in the parish record of Stratford-on-Avon that a certain child was born. There has been a movement among some of the leading actors of the world to make that day a fete day in the theatres of all nations, to make it international, so that once a year all the peoples of the earth shall be brought to think of that man who was the emperor of literature. It is just enough that this movement should come from the actors of the world, not the litterateurs, for it is to them that he belongs, not to the world of letters; that is the great and crowning glory of the stage, its one weapon against the jeers of pedantry, its one high and holy tradition, its justification before the eyes of God, that William Shakespeare was an actor, a manager, an usher even. He was not even a good or a great actor, but merely a fellow who had the dramatic instinct and hung around the theatre all his life. Not a particularly learned man and by no means a man of letters. He never knew that he was creating the literature of the future. His merry evenings at the Mermaid's Inn were never spoiled by the knowledge that the greatest savants of all nations would exhaust their wisdom to find the secret of his power. He wrote for the present, for the stage of his own day. He wrote because the theatres needed new plays and because he could construct them easily and rapidly. Some one has said that genius is the art of not taking pains. Shakespeare's genius must have been of that kind—his whole life shows it. It is not likely that he set up a great ideal and struggled to attain it. He wrote easily and carelessly, perhaps between drinks, like Dumas *père*. His best work is no more studied and premeditated than the work of God is. He wrote the truth, and it was therefore beautiful. It is doubtful if the literary excellence of his plays troubled him much. The literary critics who insist that modern actors have not sufficient intelligence to interpret Shakespeare should remember that he wrote, not for the litterateur, but for a stage infinitely lower than ours of today, and for actors infinitely less cultured. All this talk about the degradation of Shakespeare by introducing and producing his plays in modern theatres is rank nonsense. Why, if Shakespeare were alive he would think the Lansing theatre a wonderfully fine house. He would spend days of ecstasy in admiring the drops and scenery of any modern theatre. He would honestly admire much of Sardou and Dumas, and if he were to see La Grande Sarah, well, he would have nervous prostration or something very much like it. No, if Shakespeare should come to Lincoln I do not think he would be found among those occupying a chair in any of the universities. He would probably manage the Lansing, it needs a manager badly enough, heaven knows. Part of the time he would be scribbling plays over in the box office, and the rest of the time he would probably be found over at his namesake's across the street. He would possibly wear plaid trousers and a large cluster of fresh-water diamonds in his tie, just like other managers; he might even wear curly hair. Doubtless the police would run him in occasionally, just as they used to centuries ago. The cultured and the elite and the universities would know nothing at all about him, just as those of his own day knew nothing about him. Then in about two hundred years the savants the world over would begin to make pilgrimages to Lincoln and enter the Lansing on their knees.

". . . a few hungry-looking curs that have become stage-struck and have left the ordinary walks of life, cultivated a tragic howl, and seek for glory on the histrionic boards."

The Rusco & Swift *Uncle Tom's Cabin* company played that classic drama at the Lansing last night. All *Uncle Tom's Cabin* companies are bad, this being one of the worst. The companies who play the immortal production are usually made up of mongrel, nondescript actors, a very sleepy and sometimes very pretty little girl, and a few hungry-looking curs that have become stage-struck and have left the ordinary walks of life, cultivated a tragic howl, and seek for glory on the histrionic boards. These stage-struck dogs are peculiar creatures and are very much like all other actors. They are generally of plebian extraction, as their color, in spite of all their paint and "make-up," always shows. On the stage they are very fierce and courageous, but behind the flies they whine about the manager with their tail between their legs and patiently submit to the caresses of the soubrette. They are vain in the extreme and will go without their bone to wear a silver collar. They are pitiably fond of praise and pitiably sensitive to censure. If the transmigration theory is true, then surely in their previous incarnation these dramatic dogs wore checked trousers and a red tie and diamonds and walked the Rialto.

Uncle Tom's Cabin is old, older than almost any other play, because it never had enough vitality in it to keep it young. In point of construction it is about the poorest melodrama on the American stage, and that is saying a good deal. From a literary point of view the play is like the book, exaggerated, overdrawn, abounding in facts but lacking in truth. The work of a woman who sat up under cold skies of the north and tried to write of one of the warmest, richest, and most highly-colored civilizations the world has ever known; a Puritan blue-stocking who tried to blend the savage blood of the jungle and the romance of Creole civilization. The play is like the whooping cough or the measles, an experience that must be gone through with some time, and it is least painful in extreme youth.

The Rusco & Swift company is made up of an Uncle Tom who suffers from obesity, who also doubled for George Harris; an Eliza with a painful nasal twang, who also doubled for Miss Ophelia; a very wishy-washy St. Clair, a little Eva who was really very pretty and natural, and a very disgusting Topsy who wore her dresses above her knees and who must have been reading *Trilby*, as her feet and legs were very insufficiently clothed by a thin coat of black paint. I never realized until last night why Mr. Du Maurier's novel was immoral or what evil influence it could have, but that Topsy opened every eye. It is said that after the appearance of Rose in *Robert Elsmere* [by Mrs. Humphry Ward] all the young ladies in society at once began to play the violin. Now, if all the young ladies in society should begin to imitate Trilby's noted peculiarity in the matter of footwear, it would make matters awkward indeed. No, the shoe dealers cry out against the immorality of Trilby.

With these talented actors the play went along in the usual manner. Eliza crossed the river on floating ice to slow music, George Harris shot off a blank cartridge at the slave trader, Eva read Uncle Tom's words of hope and comfort about the new Jerusalem out of a city directory, and promptly at 9:45 little Eva expired, and not being interested in funerals I departed.

"Effie Ellsler, whom the program announced as 'America's greatest actress, appeared as Rosalind . . ."

Shakespeare is a strain upon the talents of the greatest actors. Why the rank and file of the profession ever attack him at all, and where they get their complacent temerity for the onslaught, is one of the unexplained mysteries. Effie Ellsler, whom the program announced as "America's greatest actress," appeared as a most pleasant and affable Rosalind at the Lansing last night. She plays that most complex and intricate of Shakespeare's lighter characters with the same regardless pleasantry which she displayed as the much married Doris last season. Certainly Miss Ellsler made a very good-natured and practical Rosalind, and certainly good nature has never been called upon to cover a greater number of artistic sins. Her voice is entirely conventional and colorless, and she continually uses that apologetic rising inflection. She chirps the most delicately shaded phrases as lightly and ineffectually and as unconscious of their significance as a sweet child of seven repeating Bible verses for butterscotch. It is amusing when it is not offensive. To hear Miss Ellsler prattle, "O, coz, my pretty coz, didst thou but know how many fathoms deep I am in love!" is an experience. Miss Ellsler's "interpretation" of the role, whatever else it may be, is certainly original. God forbid that there should be more than one woman playing it so at one time. It is a new wrinkle to enact Rosalind in a soubrette fashion, and Miss Ellsler should have all the credit of her creation. . . . Such things make one hope that Shakespeare's grave is wide and deep, and that his ghost does not walk by night.

"If a joyous elephant should break forth into song, his lay would probably be very much like Whitman's famous 'Song of Myself.' "

Speaking of monuments reminds one that there is more talk about a monument to Walt Whitman, "the good, gray poet." Just why the adjective good is always applied to Whitman it is difficult to discover, probably because people who could not understand him at all took it for granted that he meant well. If ever there was a poet who had no literary ethics at all beyond those of nature, it was he. He was neither good nor bad, any more than are the animals he continually admired and envied. He was a poet without an exclusive sense of the poetic, a man without the finer discriminations, enjoying everything with the unreasoning enthusiasm of a boy. He was the poet of the dung hill as well as of the mountains, which is admirable in theory but excruciating in verse. In the same paragraph he informs you that, "The pure contralto sings in the organ loft," and that "The malformed limbs are tied to the table, what is removed drop horribly into a pail." No branch of surgery is poetic, and that hopelessly prosaic word "pail" would kill a whole volume of sonnets. Whitman's poems are reckless rhapsodies over creation in general, sometimes sublime, sometimes ridiculous. He declares that the ocean with its "imperious waves, commanding" is beautiful, and that the fly-specks on the walls are also beautiful. Such catholic taste may go in science, but in poetry their results are sad. The poet's task is usually to select the poetic. Whitman never bothers to do that, he takes everything in the universe from fly-specks to the fixed stars. His *Leaves of Grass* is a sort of dictionary of the English language, and in it is the name of everything in creation set down with great reverence but without any particular connection.

But however ridiculous Whitman may be there is a primitive elemental force about him. He is so full of hardiness and of the joy of life. He looks at all nature in the delighted, admiring way in which the old Greeks and the primitive poets did. He exults so in the red blood in his body and the strength in his arms. He has such a passion for the warmth and dignity of all that is natural. He has no code but to be natural, a code that this complex world has so long outgrown. He is sensual, not after the manner of Swinburne and Gautier, who are always seeking for perverted and bizarre effects on the senses, but in the frank fashion of the old barbarians who ate and slept and married and smacked their lips over the mead horn. He is rigidly limited to the physical, things that quicken his pulses, please his eyes, or delight his nostrils. There is an element of poetry in all this, but it is by no means the highest. If a joyous elephant should break forth into song, his lay would probably be very much like Whitman's famous "Song of Myself." It would have just about as much delicacy and deftness and discrimination. He says: "I think I could turn and live with the animals. They are so placid and self-contained, I stand and look at them long and long. They do not sweat and whine about their condition. They do not lie awake in the dark and weep for their sins. They do not make me sick discussing their duty to God. Not one is dissatisfied nor not one is demented with the mania of many things. Not one kneels to another nor to his kind that lived thousands of years ago. Not one is respectable or unhappy, over the whole earth." And that is not irony on nature, he means just that, life meant no more to him. He accepted the world just as it is and glorified it, the seemly and the unseemly, the good and the bad. He had no conception of a difference in people or in things. All men had bodies and were alike to him, one about as good as another. To live was to fulfil all natural laws and impulses. To be comfortable was to be happy. To be happy was the ultimatum. He did not realize the existence of a conscience or a responsibility. He had no more thought of good or evil than the folks in Kipling's *Jungle Book*.

And yet there is an undeniable charm about this optimistic vagabond who is made happy by the warm sunshine and the smell of spring fields. A sort of good fellowship and wholeheartedness in every line he wrote. His veneration for things physical and material, for all that is in water or air or land, is so real that as you read him you think for the moment that you would rather like to live so if you could. For the time you half believe that a sound body and a strong arm are the greatest things in the world. Perhaps no book shows so much as *Leaves of Grass* that keen senses do not make a poet. When you read it you realize how spirited a thing poetry really is and how great a part spiritual perceptions play in apparently sensuous verse, if only to select the beautiful from the gross.

Fringe Benefits

By WILLIAM K. ZINSSER

I am not one of your common cranks who hate to make out an income-tax form at this time of year. True, there's a certain drudgery in computing my "credit from tax-free covenant bonds" and determining whether I am eligible for "annuities under the Railroad Retirement Act." (I can never remember when I last retired a railroad.) But this is a small price to pay for the thrill, every April, of listing my contributions to charity. How brightly the taxable year still glows in the rearview mirror of Form 1040. For charity no longer begins at home, alone with a pen and a checkbook. Today, giving money to a worthy cause is a perpetual lark, and I have my check stubs to prove it.

To think, for instance (Hadley Home for Unmarried Mothers, $38), that my wife and I would have missed the "Hoboken Grape Festival" if "Dee-Dee" Page hadn't been on the benefit committee. Dee-Dee remembered how much we had enjoyed her "Boxwood Tour of Darien" when she was raising money for Crowther College, and as soon as I saw her handwriting across the top of the pink brochure—"This'll be a fun benefit, hope you can join Herb and me"—I knew we wouldn't be disappointed.

We weren't. Dee-Dee had hired an old-fashioned ferryboat to take us over to Hoboken, and that was a treat to begin with. And then of course there was the festival itself: all those picturesque Old World types treading on the grapes and singing folk songs that they had learned as children in Andorra—and all within sight of the towers of Manhattan! That was well worth $25.

Or take the terribly clever benefit (Pets Anonymous, $36) that George and "Miffy" Tremaine held for their psychotherapy clinic for dis-

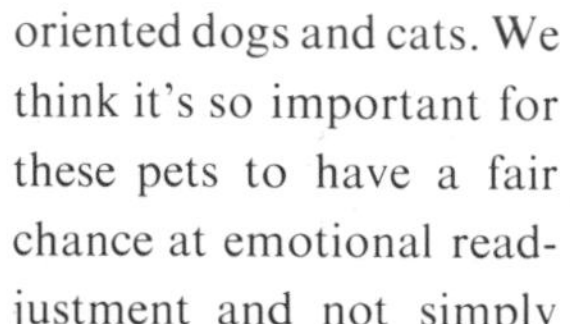

oriented dogs and cats. We think it's so important for these pets to have a fair chance at emotional readjustment and not simply be chloroformed (or worse), and yet the previous fund appeal, which was simply a request for money, had left us vaguely unsatisfied. But last year George and Miffy went all out when they took over El Morocco for one night and turned it into a giant doghouse. You entered on all fours, and the waiters were dogs dressed up in jackets, who served hors d'oeuvres in the shape of Ken-L-Ration biscuits. That really dramatized how appealing dogs can be when they're given a break in this thoughtless world.

What we had come to see, however, was the program of "Great Animal Scenes From Hollywood," and for pure enjoyment it repaid us every nickel of the two tickets at $27.50 apiece ($18 deductible). There was the whole gang up on the screen—Rin-Tin-Tin, Lassie, Silver, Trigger, Francis the mule, Rhubarb the cat, Samantha the duck in *Friendly Persuasion*, and many more. We could have watched them all night. Come to think of it, we did.

And speaking of Samantha, there wasn't any way to duck the organ-loft tour (Scola Gregoria, $24) that the Witherspoons dreamed up for "the Scola," which is a choir that specializes in liturgical music of the ninth century (A.D.). Harry and "Moo-Moo" know that I'm a music buff—they've often heard me say that the motets of the ninth century are better than the eighth- and tenth-century stuff (funny how those things go in cycles)—and heaven knows, if people like us don't support these societies they'll die out altogether.

Still, the Witherspoons have had a hard time competing for "the charity dollar," and quite frankly I think they would have given up the fight last year if they hadn't hit upon a visit to the organ lofts of the dozen biggest churches in New York. The idea of having each host organist serve punch from out of the pipes was a cute touch, and I, for one, don't even remember climbing to the "great wind chamber" of St. Bartholomew's. That's how good it was.

But for me the best kind of benefit is a costume ball. My tax records show that we went to twenty-seven during the year, and every one was different. I mean you just can't compare—to take a few at random—the "Moonlight Mazurka" (Chopin House Scholarship Fund, $22), the "First Half-Century Hornpipe" (Follansbee Sailors' Home, $18), the "Roaring Twenties Maxixe" (Old Stutzville Auto Museum, $22), the "Hoot Mon Highland Fling" (Presbyterian Missions in Botswana, $25), and the "Quarto Quadrille" (Globe-Theatre-in-Flushing, Inc., $20). Each was fun in its own way, not even counting the good times we had thinking of what to wear.

Looking back, I guess the only benefit that I didn't want to attend was the "Pipes & Sewers Promenade" under the streets of Manhattan (Friends of the Dig at Wadi-el-Misr, $28). But we couldn't very well get out of it because it's the favorite charity of Frank and "Pootie" Prendergast, and they took tickets to *my* favorite charity, Bundles for Bursitis. (As a matter of fact, I think we gave them a real treat by getting the final preview to the musical *Valley Forge!* just one night before the Broadway opening, because when it *did* open it only ran four performances and they would have missed Giles Gentry's stunning tenor soliloquy, "The Endless Winter.")

Anyway, I certainly didn't begrudge the Prendergasts the $28 for their dig at Wadi-el-Misr, because the eleven shards that Professor Zapf found there in 1964 more than justify his "hunch" that it's the long-lost site of Pre-Iraqi B, which everyone has been looking for since Stoddard found Pre-Iraqi A. Finally I *made* myself take the "Pipes & Sewers" tour, and I've got to admit it was fascinating, not to mention how vividly it promoted the whole idea of archaeology.

The tour began around 8:30 P.M. at a hole in Fifth Avenue at 57th Street. We went down one of those little repairmen's ladders and were met at the bottom by Dr. Stickney, who holds the chair of Subterranean Engineering at Fordham. What a spellbinding guide he turned out to be. The time went so quickly that when we came back up, around 11, we were at Riverside Drive and 113th Street. Hats off to Frank and "Pootie," I say.

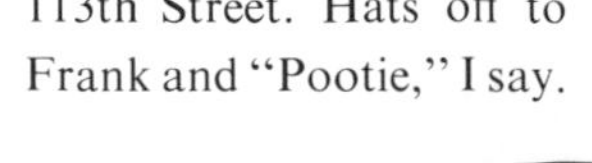